Anjani Kumar Singh was born in 1958 in Siwan district of Bihar but he spent his childhood in Chamtha village of Begusarai. He did his graduation from Patna University and his post-graduation from Jawaharlal Nehru University, New Delhi, and has an MBA from Southern Cross University, Australia. He joined the Indian Administrative Service in 1981 in the Bihar cadre. He held the post of District Magistrate of Santhal Pargana (Dumka) and Vaishali districts and was posted as Divisional Commissioner Purnia. After working as Director in the then Union Ministry of Human Resource Development and Social Empowerment, he served as Secretary in the Health, Education, Finance, Art, Culture and Youth departments of the Government of Bihar. He was also posted as Principal Secretary to the Chief Minister, and Chief Secretary of Bihar. At present, he is posted as Advisor to the Chief Minister and Director General of the Bihar Museum. His interests include horticulture, art, culture and women's empowerment.

One Life Is Enough

Anjani Kumar Singh

SPEAKING TIGER BOOKS LLP
4381/4, Ansari Road, Daryaganj
New Delhi 110002

First published by Speaking Tiger Books in paperback in 2023

Copyright © Anjani Kumar Singh 2023

ISBN 978-93-5447-570-2
eISBN 978-93-5447-494-1

10 9 8 7 6 5 4 3 2 1

All rights reserved.
No part of this publication may be reproduced, transmitted, or stored in a retrieval system, in any form or by any means, electronic, mechanical, photocopying, recording or otherwise, without the prior permission of the publisher.

This book is sold subject to the condition that it shall not, by way of trade or otherwise, be lent, resold, hired out, or otherwise circulated, without the publisher's prior consent, in any form of binding or cover other than that in which it is published.

For my wife Poornima, daughter Apurva Srishti and son Apurva Sukant, and my fellow travellers.

Contents

Acknowledgements	ix
1. Childhood Days	1
2. Memories of Patna College and the Jayaprakash Narayan Movement	17
3. JNU and the IAS	25
4. The Journey from One District to Another	43
5. Five Years at the Centre	106
6. From Sachivalaya to the Chief Minister's Office	117
7. Memory Bank	183
8. The World Before Me	188
9. In the World of Culture and Horticulture	244
10. Friends Forever	253

Acknowledgements

I first wrote my memoir in Hindi and it was published with the title *Kaafi Hai Ek Zindagi* in early 2022. It has taken a while to translate and publish the book in English, and I hope this edition will find new readers and that it will interest them. I'm grateful to Jerry Pinto, Sharanya Awasthi and the Speaking Tiger editorial team for their help with the English translation.

1
Childhood Days

Every person has a story. That story will often feature a village and in that village, a home. My story, being no different, starts with my village, Chamtha. It is extraordinary in one respect: it is so large that it has two panchayats and sprawls across three political districts of the Lok Sabha and the Vidhan Sabha. Chamtha stands at the sangam (confluence) of four districts: Patna, Samastipur, Begusarai and Vaishali. My home is in the Bachhwara block of the Begusarai region. As it was the epicentre of four districts, the root of its name must lie in the notion: 'chau' (four) 'math' (head). Words wear out with use. Chaumath too must have worn out and eventually turned into Chamtha.

To the south of Chamtha flows the Ganga; to the north, the Baya. Every year, some of the land on the banks of the Ganga is swallowed up and emerges on the south side. This is why some of the land of Chamtha lies in the Patna block. The phenomena of the land vanishing in this way and reappearing on the other side are known as *Gang-shikast* and *Gang-baraar* respectively.

Our ancestors migrated from Ajmer in Rajasthan about 150 years ago. We are Chauhan Rajputs and still perform pooja in honour of the deceased members of our family on a hill in the city of Ajmer. When my ancestors first arrived here, they settled in a village called Kashtahara, about two kilometres from Chamtha. The land was fertile here, far more than in Rajasthan. As the family grew, it spread out as members began to settle in the surrounding villages. Four generations ago, one branch of the family settled in Chamtha. As this area was sparsely inhabited, land was freely available. In this district, sugarcane, maize and wheat grew well, which brought prosperity to farmers.

The Baya River flows in front of our home. A bridge spans the river and has its own story. There is an area called Narhan in the adjoining district where people came to bathe at the time of Karthik, which falls in the months of November/December. A queen of Narhan would come every year to perform this Karthik-snaan on the Chamtha Ghat. Each time she had to cross the river by boat which was inconvenient for a royal personage. In order to avoid this inconvenience and to make the passage across the river easier for the locals, she ordered a bridge to be built across the river. Lakhs of people still come to take a holy dip at Kartik. There is also a big fair at the same time.

The most important place near my village is Vidyapatinagar. It has a huge temple dedicated to Lord Shankar. There is a folk tale about the great poet Vidyapati. It is said that in his old age, Vidyapati decided that he wanted to offer his body to the Ganga. He travelled up to the place now called Vidyapatinagar. Then it occurred to him that if he had come so far in order to achieve his desire to offer his body to the Ganga, should Mother Ganga not travel at least this much to help her devotee fulfil his wishes? The story goes that the river obliged.

There is another famous story about Mahakavi Vidyapati. It is said that Vidyapati always had a servitor called Ugna with him. One day, he was very thirsty but Ugna was nowhere around. Vidyapati began to seek him desperately. And suddenly, there was Ugna with water, water that was actually Gangajal. Vidyapati quenched his thirst and Ugna vanished. It is said that this was not Ugna but Lord Shankar himself. Impressed by Vidyapati's love and devotion, the Lord had taken the form of his servant.

The majority of the people in my village are farmers from the Yadav and the Rajput communities. Wheat, corn, tobacco, chillies, sugarcane and other vegetables flourish there. Agriculture and animal husbandry are the chief occupations. Milk goes out to be sold. Since Chamtha is located between two rivers, fishing also occurs on a grand scale. Annual floods would submerge the fields and the houses of the poor. There were many who had their homes at the edge of the river and they had even more trouble. And so, the villagers would store food grains, firewood and other essentials in advance for the two months of the floods. Vegetables would also be dried and stored. Mangoes would be made into amavat (mango flap).

Our family placed great emphasis on education and so its members joined the army, the police or took up other government jobs. In fact, the Rajput community as a whole, which already owned much land, focused on acquiring an education as well and so it became prosperous over time. Our family began to be counted as one of the wealthy ones in the area. This gave us some political and economic status, but over a period of time things began to change and other, disprivileged, castes also began to show interest in farming and education.

The upper class and castes did not have the same level of industriousness and so the land eventually ended up in the hands of the farmers who worked all by themselves in the fields. The other difference was that the upper-caste women did not work in the fields and so half the workforce was locked up in the house. This was not a problem for the so-called lower castes. Their entire families worked on the land and their children sought for work in cities and towns, which increased their income.

The majority of the village land was owned by the Rajputs. Many of them were very rich. But over time, the land began to be sold since they seemed prone to bad habits and many were not industrious. This land was bought by the Yadavs and the Kushwahas who grew vegetables on it. In my childhood, I saw that many farmers with extensive property would settle families on the land to till it. Once they were settled on the land, the landowner had the right to demand their labour. These families ended up in debt for some reason or the other. Sometimes it was a daughter's marriage, at other times, an illness in the family. The interest rates were extortionate. There was a large book covered in red cloth called the pustika in which both capital and interest were noted. Once your name was entered into the book, it was not likely that you could erase it in your lifetime. The relationship between the landowner and the labourer was very strange. On one side was the guarantee that the essential labour of the fields would never stop but on the other, it was also true that they were tied forever to their lord and master.

Each home had a boat or two in which one went out to defecate when the village was submerged by floods. I had a great affinity for all things natural: for water, for the river and fish. We had our own boat in which I also went out to patrol the fields.

We also practised a ritual called *jhijhari*. On certain nights, we would carry our food on to the boat and take it out on to the water. The women would sing songs. Sailing on moonlit nights was a wonderful experience. The calmness of the hour, the gentleness of the night breeze and the sounds of women singing in unison, the fresh, cool breeze and beneath us the quiet lapping of the water all combined to transport my childish mind to another world altogether.

The people of the village had learnt to live with the floods. To protect their homes, they would build barricades made out of banana stalks. This broke the impact of the floodwaters. The water sources, including wells would be submerged during the floods. Water had to be boiled before it could be drunk. This was a time of rice-and-fish meals for the poor because the supply of fish was plentiful and cheap. There was another benefit to the floods: new soil would be brought down by the water and a layer of fertile soil would be spread over the fields. This ensured a good rabi crop of wheat, for instance, and there would be no need for any chemical fertilisers. Now there is a dam between my village and the Ganga and so the floods have been reduced. There are generally three crops across the entire district these days.

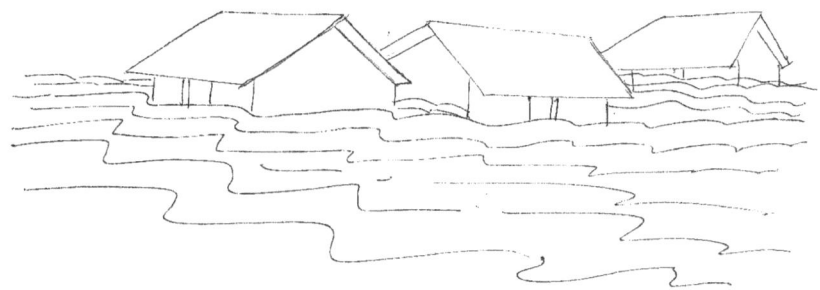

In Bihar, as in the rest of rural India, there was a shortage of government village schools. The government schools were in the big cities or towns, which meant that children had to travel long distances every day. Thus, many schools were started by the local population.

The rich would often establish and support these schools. Some would donate land; others would pay for the building or contribute in other ways. The teachers were drawn from the surrounding areas; they would combine teaching with their traditional family occupations. In some areas, wealthy people would set up schools in the name of their fathers or grandfathers. The primary and high schools started by the leading citizens of the area would be run by committees composed of the prominent residents of the area. Since the committees and the teachers belonged to the place, they carried out their duties with a greater sense of responsibility. Over a period of time, the state government began to acquire these schools. Once this happened, the teachers became government employees and although their salaries rose, there was a decline in their commitment to society and, inevitably, the quality of education diminished.

I studied at the Vidyapati High School which had been established by public donations. The school then ran on the support of the general public. A management committee was in charge of it. The school was about three kilometres from my home. I had a cycle to go to school which was a luxury; at that time, very few people owned cycles. There was a management committee in charge of the school. Along with the usual round of academics, we were required to do an hour of shramdaan (social service) every week. The children would either carry bricks for the school building or they would clean up the playground and the gardens. Thanks to the public support it received, the school eventually boasted a large, beautiful building. Later, the school was taken over by the government. The school organized sports, debates and essay competitions so that the children would get an all-round education. In those days, one had to choose whether one was going to read the humanities or the sciences in the seventh or eighth standard. Everyone wanted me to study science but I did not like mathematics. So I chose the humanities. I passed my matriculation from this school.

The matriculation exam is an important milestone in the life of every student. Admission to a good college is based on the score a student achieves, as is the right to study the subject of one's choice. I worked very hard to score high marks in the matric exam. All of us studied on our own but some boys got together and met every evening and tested each other on various subjects. The Bihar University School Examinations Committee conducted the matriculation examination for the entire State of Bihar. Regardless of which school you went to, every student sat for the same exam. It was also the tradition that students would not sit for the exam in their own school but go to another. I sat for my papers in a school that was fifteen kilometres away from my village. The exam lasted for a full week and so the candidates would often make arrangements for their stay with their local guardian or in a relative's home. The exam was held in winter so we went fully prepared. My exam went well and I scored 72 per cent, which was very good in those days. And since I had scored well, I was admitted to the best Arts college in Bihar—Patna College. Thus, I got the opportunity to leave the village and study in the city, which made my family very happy.

I was the goalkeeper of the school's football team. Our team was better than most of the others in the area. Some of our players represented the district too. Our school celebrated Saraswati Pooja with great pomp. Durga Pooja was also celebrated on a grand scale on the neighbouring grounds. In those days, the Ram-Leela would run over several nights. We would wrap up in warm clothes and enjoy the performance late into the night. At that time, the female parts were also played by men.

During my school days, I was addicted to reading detective novels. Stories featuring characters such as colonel Vinod and Captain Hamid were very popular. I found these books unputdownable. I would even carry them to school, concealed among my exercise books, to read during the recess. My mother knew of this habit and she was concerned that I spent more time with these books than with my school texts. When she called me for a meal and I was late in responding, she knew that I was engrossed in a detective novel. One day, she spotted a text book that looked rather swollen. She asked me to show it to her and found a novel concealed inside. She then asked me whether I went to school to study or to read jasoosi (detective) novels. If this was what I wanted to do, why bother going to school? After that I stopped carrying these books to school and satisfied my craving by reading them at night.

Although my mother was a disciplinarian and stern on the outside, she was very kind to children. Once we were celebrating Holi at our house and all through the village. Everyone was playing with colours while I was in bed with a high fever. I was on a strict diet of barley water. The entire house was filled with the aroma of dishes being cooked. I was lying in bed, depressed, when my mother came up to me carrying a thali (plate) of malpua and other sweets. She said, 'Go on, this much will not harm you.' I was overjoyed and that day, I saw her compassionate side.

At that time, we would get a chavanni (four-anna) coin every day as pocket-money to spend in school. Four annas equals twenty-five paise. When we had a break, we would buy snacks to eat. It was not the tradition, in those days, to take a tiffin box from home to school. There was a small shop outside the school which sold things like mudi, chivda, pakodis and other sweets and savouries. Four annas got you so much food that you could share the spoils with your friends. Later, there was a film song on the chavanni, which became very popular. Today, the four-anna coin has been demonetized.

I was born in the police quarters of Raghunathpur, Siwan district in 1958, but I spent all my childhood in Chamtha. My father, the late Ramraj Singh, was a police officer and at the time of my birth, had been posted in Raghunathpur. My mother, Shivdularidevi, was a home maker. I was the second of four brothers and a sister. My elder brother, the late Ashwani Kumar Singh, was a farmer in the village.

Most people in our village lived in joint families. There were many reasons for this. Not only did it save costs because food was cooked together, it also provided a sense of security. Everyone had different roles to play and the head of the family was responsible for all the needs of the family members. Everyone was expected to do what their skills and talent would allow. Some worked in the land and some held down jobs. Those who had jobs knew that their children would be well looked after in the joint family. There was no need to make separate arrangements for them. If a member of the family was working in the city, it was understood that a younger member of the family—a sibling, cousin, niece or nephew—who had got admission in the city college would stay with him/her.

We also lived in a joint family. My father was one of three brothers. Two brothers lived in the village. By today's standards, we had a peculiar system. Children lived and studied with their paternal uncles, not with their parents.

This meant that there was a lot of love in the family. Because of this system, though my father worked in the city and my mother lived with him, I lived and studied in the village with my uncles. It was not considered right to show too much love for one's own children. My eldest uncle, who was known to all as Babuji, was the head of the house. However, he was not in charge of the finances; the money handled by my second-eldest uncle, who everyone knew as Dada. Lala, who was Dada's son, lived and studied with my father. Since we were a joint family, there were any number of children around. And so there was cooperation and love among us which also provided us with the power of unity. It seems to me that people in those days were not selfish and did not focus on their own children's success to the exclusion of all else. People raised in such families, in my opinion, took greater interest in social causes.

We had a high school teacher who lived with us. His name was Phulendra Narain Singh. By day, he taught us in the school and in the evenings, he taught us at home. When we had finished playing, we washed up and sang 'Raghupati Raghava Raja Ram' and then sat down to study. We gathered in a circle around a lantern. There were images of great men on the walls of our home; these included Mahatma Gandhi and Jawaharlal Nehru. We also had a step-brother called Vijay, who was not very interested in his studies. I remember he would begin to doze off when we were studying. Guruji was a strict teacher. He had a row of canes hanging on the wall. We had another beloved teacher—Ramchandra Mishra Prabhakar who was from Rosda, Samastipur. He improved our Hindi. On Sunday evenings, we had readings from the Ramayana. All the parva festivals were celebrated.

The teachers who lived with us were like members of the family. They would weigh in on every important decision the family made. Babuji was tall, well-built and a quiet man who was very popular among the children. Dada was much stricter and if we played about too much in the mud, we would get it from him. One of the good things about that time was that even if one of the farmhands came and complained about some mischief that we had done, it would be taken seriously. An inquiry would be conducted and we would be beaten.

I was a good student so I was given a separate room to study and live. I had a radio in my room which was the most popular form of mass entertainment. We listened to many songs on the radio and waited impatiently each week for Binaca Geetmala. Most of our family members were non-vegetarians but there was a separate fireplace and a separate space for cooking these items. In those days, we did not cook eggs or chicken. Since I liked eggs, I got the family doctor to tell my uncle that I should have an egg every day so that I might study well. In those days, there was also a tonic called Phosphomin which was supposed to make your brain sharp. I was given this to drink as well. Since we could not cook eggs at home, they were boiled in a separate kettle out in the garden. At that time, Hindus did not keep chickens.

The rate for daily labour was then two rupees or two seers of grain. But there were many labourers—such as the barber, the blacksmith, or the carpenter—who were not paid in cash. However, they got a share in the crop. When vegetables or fruits which we had grown were brought home, the first fruits went to the Brahmins. At that time, if you met a Brahmin on the road or at home, you had to bow before him even if he was younger. I always found this surprising. The practice of untouchability was widespread but it was beginning to fade away slowly. The new generation of students who were studying in school and college did not pay much attention to untouchability. They played with children of all communities.

There was a tradition in our home that one learned to use firearms at an early age. We generally shot birds and that was how we learned marksmanship. How much land you owned and how many firearms you had were markers of your position in the hierarchy. We were one of the ten land-owning and wealthy families of the area. My two stepbrothers began to work before I did. One of them even helped us financially during the time I was in college and my father had passed away.

The majority of the children in my school had not seen a big city nor had they travelled by train. Pitaji, who was in the police service, was generally posted in the cities. I would go and visit him during the vacations and so I had travelled by train and by car among other means of transport. When I went to visit my parents, my mother would lovingly cook khasti for me. I watched a lot of films when I went to the city. When I returned to the village, I would tell my classmates the stories of these films, accompanied by suitable actions.

I have many memories of my father. We never spoke to him directly. Or you might say, we never looked him in the eye and spoke to him. Whatever we wanted to tell him would be told to Mother or through a friend. Unless he called us to him, we did not seek him out. After he had a meal, he would enjoy a cigarette but I didn't like the smell of cigarettes then, nor do I like it now. He had become a vegetarian but did not object to anyone else eating meat at the same table.

My father was a tall, strapping man. He was a good volleyball player. I would often get the opportunity to play with him. Once, we were playing volleyball together and there were about ten or fifteen minutes left for the match to end. The Superintendent of Police (SP) arrived at the police station. Pitaji kept on playing. Only when he had finished the game did he go to meet the SP.

Pitaji had made arrangements to support a talented child from an underprivileged family. When he was posted in Muzaffarpur in Bihar, this student came to live with us. He was treated as a member of the family and lived with us until he finished his education and then joined the office of the Accountant General.

When my father was an inspector with the railways, I got the opportunity to travel first class air-conditioned on the Danapur-Howdah train. He was a devotee of Lord Shankara. Wherever he went, he got a temple built. He was responsible for getting temples built in Bonka and Sahalgaon. When he was posted in Muzaffarpur, he would visit the temple at Garibsthan. He would also go to the Muslim mazaar (dargah) that was close by. A spiritually inclined man, he was not narrow-minded or bigoted in the least. He would generally go to the temple in the evenings for a spell of meditation.

Once, it so happened that my elder brother failed the year. He was not interested in studying. Any other guardian would have given him a beating. But to encourage his son, Pitaji recited a popular sher (couplet):

Girte hain shasavaar hi maidan-e jung mein
Tifl kya girega jo gutne ke bal chale?

(It is only the mounted soldier who falls in battle.
Who can fall if he is already on his knees?)

My father was a kindly man, always ready to lend the poor a helping hand. I remember a boy in our area who was very good at his studies. He was from a very poor family. His father eked out a living by selling milk. My father helped the boy to complete his education. Later, he went on to become an audit officer.

2

Memories of Patna College and the Jayaprakash Narayan Movement

After I finished my matriculation in the village, I applied to Patna College. I was admitted into the Intermediate course. The admission list and the timetable were put up together. I remember my first day clearly. On the very first day, I made five or six friends and I have remained close to them.

Patna College's humanities department was well-known. The best students of Bihar took admission there. On the walls was a notice, 'The Best in Bihar are from Patna College', which filled us with pride. We were after all students of Patna University, which was referred to as the Oxford of the East then. I was allotted a room in Jackson Hostel.

I was in college in 1974 when Jayaprakash Narayan's 'Total Revolution' movement unfolded in Bihar. It sought immediate change in education, governance and society as a whole. Jayaprakash Narayan, popularly known as JP, had experienced the British Raj and studied abroad. At first, he was a leftist but he joined the Congress Party later, and the socialists thereafter. Mahatma Gandhi left a deep impression on his life. His wife, Prabhavati ji, was a disciple of Mahatma Gandhi. Together with Ram Manohar Lohia, JP was the main pillar of socialist thought, and he was even more influential than Vinobha Bhave.

The youth in those days saw an urgent need for reform in spheres such as education, the political dispensation and the societal structure. JP understood that change could be brought about by harnessing the energy of the youth. He gave a call for a transformative social revolution, which he named 'Total Revolution'. Many students and young people answered the call and joined the movement. I too joined it.

I was about sixteen or seventeen, an Intermediate student. I heard many of JP's speeches at Patna's Gandhi Maidan and participated in his rallies. The JP Movement spread rapidly through Patna University and then throughout the State and reached other States as well. As students, we held meetings in our hostels and worked out strategies to hasten the spread of the revolution. And then the Centre declared a national emergency and all the leaders of the movement were arrested. But the news had spread and some leaders went underground and kept the movement going. As students, we decided to take the movement to the villages, we were keen that all of us should return to our villages and spread the word there. With a couple of my classmates, I too went back to my village, Chamtha. For two days, we talked to the students and the youth, explaining the meaning of 'Total Revolution' and enlisting them in the movement. The JP Movement thus went to the villages and was a huge success.

My family was aware of my involvement in the movement and offered no opposition to it. They knew there were some rotten apples in the basket, but they were also aware that almost the entire student community was taking part in the movement. At least tacitly, our elders supported the movement.

At the meeting in our hostel, it was also decided that we would no longer participate in the educational system as it existed and that we would boycott the university examinations. This oath to boycott the examinations was taken by all the students in front of the Patna College by the banks of the Ganga. The Intermediate examination was announced and all of us stayed away.

But one or two students from my hostel sat for the exam. This enraged the others. Some students from B.N. College came to the hostel to beat up a student from Patna College who had written his papers. We had a strange attitude then. While we might be angry with the student who had sat for the exams, we were certainly not going to let someone from another college beat him up. We intercepted the boys from B.N. College and told them that we would punish the betrayer appropriately.

Since very few students had given the examination, this boy stood first. Later, he joined the Indian Administrative Service (IAS) and became one of the chief officers of the Bihar cadre.

We were now on the horns of a dilemma. The majority of us had not written the examinations and so further studies were out of the question. Eventually Patna held a supplementary examination for us. All of us wrote this exam and so we passed the Intermediate level.

Jayaprakash Narayan had a charismatic personality. His life was marked by a beautiful simplicity. He was an effective speaker. His dream of 'Total Revolution' inspired the student community. The youth were desperate for change and so JP was extremely popular among them. We would go to Gandhi Maidan in Patna to hear him speak. Some of the students who were involved in the JP Movement began to participate in mainstream political activities as well. Later, they would hold important political posts at the State and national level. JP's was a revolution in thought, a philosophical revolution which sought to distance itself from violence.

Once the police used tear gas shells on a student meeting at the Patna University campus. The students were ready. They caught the tear gas shells in wet towels and lobbed them back at the police. After this, there was a raid on the hostel. We locked ourselves in our rooms. The police managed to open the shutters of some of the rooms and threw the tear-gas shells in. We were trained for this and we dumped them in buckets of water until they ran out. All this took place under the supervision of a police officer called R.D. Suvarno. Later, when I joined the IAS and went to Hazaribagh as Circle Officer, R.D. Suvarno was Reserve Officer at Ramgarh Police Circle.

We had heard that if the police put you in jail, you would get a pair of Jubilee chappals, a lungi and a shawl. Ten of us from Jackson Hostel thus courted jail. The administration there knew full well why we were there. They gave us our Jubilee chappals and our shawls. We returned to the hostel late in the night.

The student unions were also active in Patna University. At that time, there were two factions: on one side were the Rajputs and the Kurmis. On the other, the Bhumihars and the Yadavs, etc. The majority of the students were Yadavs. Later I would discover the secret of this equation; it became clear to me that the geographic spread of caste in the State had something to do with it. Generally, Rajputs and Yadavs were to be found in the same areas; and where there were Bhumihars, there were Kurmis. Initially, the heads of the unions were always Rajputs or Bhumihars. But later, the lower castes began to realize that they had the strength of numbers and were no longer satisfied with posts like General Secretary. They wanted to be President and so it came to pass.

All the good students wanted to study at Patna University. Its atmosphere was generally conducive to learning. However, from time to time, there would be outbreaks of caste-based violence. There were also occasional fights between rival student unions and competing colleges. Once there was a cricket match between Jackson Hostel and Minto Hostel and a fight broke out in the middle of the match. We began to beat up the Minto boys with the sticks taken from the mosquito nets. Some of the boys were caught in the middle of the fight by a police inspector from Pirbahor who was patrolling there. As they were herded into the police jeep, the young men began to weep. Later, the police inspector made them promise to abstain from violence and even fed them sweetmeats.

In the evenings, we would wander around Patna Market. I was addicted to paan from childhood. I come from Mithila where we welcome guests with paan supari. The women ate paan too. When I was called upon to serve a guest, I would pop some into my mouth. By the ninth or tenth class, I was eating zarda with my paan. By the time I was in Patna College, my daily routine included rinsing my mouth with gul manjan and then eating paan. Rinsing with gul manjan has its own thrill. When I went to Delhi on deputation, I dropped the paan habit; there were no spittoons and one could not disrupt meetings to go out and spit.

I replaced the habit with Paan Paraag and zarda which continues to this day.

During our college days, we would sometimes take bhang. Once I succumbed to the intoxication. Generally, I would eat three rotis for dinner but that night, I ate six or seven and kept laughing. My friends realized something was wrong and took me to the Patna Medical College Hospital (PCMH). There, the doctor stripped the hide off me. He said that our parents had sent us to college to study and here we were living lives of dissolution.

Under the influence of the bhang, I began to worry what would happen if I died of an overdose. What would my parents think? A worthy death might have been fighting for the Motherland after joining the army. This idea would not leave my head. Anyway, the doctor mixed an emetic in water and gave it to me to drink. I vomited copiously and finally the effect wore off.

At that time, it was quite the fashion among the thuggish students to carry knives. I too had a fine knife. When we stopped going to college because of the JP Movement, there was a faction of students which wanted the exams postponed. I was the leader of this group. There were other students who opposed this. When we were returning from the office of the Vice-Chancellor after presenting our memorandum, we met our opponents. Most of them ran off when they saw how many of us were there. However, their leader stood his ground and got into it with me. I pulled out my knife but as I was about to slash at him, one of my friends stayed my hand. Later, this young man became my good friend and joined the police force.

I did my BA (Hons) in geography from Patna College. The syllabus was based on Oxford University's.

The standards of teaching were high. There were famous teachers like Professor P. Dayal and Professor Inayat Ahmed there. Professor Rasbehari Singh had joined a few years earlier. My favourite teachers, including Professor L.N. Ram and Dr Rasbehari Singh who made a significant contribution towards the study of history, developed interesting ways of teaching the subject; they wanted to liberate history from the realm of academe and bring it out into the streets where an understanding of the past might help the process of building a better future.

The hostel was emptied because of the JP Movement. I left Jackson Hostel and went to stay with a classmate, Kashinath Shukla, who had rented rooms in Bhikhna Pahadi Mohalla. Once, I was playing cards with another friend, Ranveer, when we saw Surendra Bhagat approaching. Bhagat would top the Science College and I, Patna College. Generally, the Best Graduate Prize would go to the Science College. The decision was based on the total scores of the Pass course and the Honours course. That day the results had been declared. I thought Bhagat was coming to tell us of his being chosen as the Best Graduate. Instead, he said that I had won that honour. My subjects were geography and political science. I had scored high marks right from the Intermediate level and had consistently topped my college but I had never expected to become Best Graduate.

Now it was time to bid farewell to Patna College. Our juniors organized a farewell for us. As I entered the hall, chewing paan, my glance fell upon a young woman. She smiled and I smiled back at her.

Who knew that four or five years later, Poornima—for that was her name, would end up becoming my wife? After that first meeting, we did meet once or twice about class notes.

In those days, the toppers of Patna University would receive job offers from banks. Kashinath Shukla of Bhikhna Pahadi Mohalla told me later that such a letter had indeed come for me. How different my life would have been had I taken a bank job then!

When I went to Delhi for further studies, my professors at Patna asked why. As a university topper, I could get a lecturer's job in Patna. At that time the Vice-Chancellor had the power to appoint lecturers but I was on my way. In 1977–78, I joined Jawaharlal Nehru University (JNU). One year later, Poornima joined JNU too. She too broke with tradition, being a free spirit who wanted to live life on her own terms.

3

JNU and the IAS

The JP Movement had affected Patna University's reputation negatively, and so, many Bihari students decided to come to Delhi for higher education. This was the first time that a large number of students from Bihar had arrived in Delhi. The majority joined JNU or Delhi University (DU). Based on my performance, I secured admission in the Delhi School of Economics of DU which offered good hostel accommodation. But I sat for the JNU entrance test and was selected for the Centre of Regional Development with geography as my subject.

JNU was not your run-of-the-mill university; it was and remains one of its kind. Established in 1969, it was a unique educational experiment, meant to bring together teachers and students from different parts of the country so as to conduct research into the many and varied aspects of knowledge. It was based on international models and admissions were conducted through an entrance test, but some weightage was also given to students from disadvantaged backgrounds. This meant that many of the students in JNU were from underprivileged States or underprivileged families. Since it was run on international lines, it provided its students with a huge canvas on which were inscribed many cultures, languages and customs. At its base, it was a residential university and so the students who came there experienced the belongingness of living in a diverse and heterogenous national family, and even an international family. They had the opportunity to listen to and understand each other, and since they came from different backgrounds, they evolved intellectually and emotionally because of these interactions.

In the beginning, leftist and socialist thought predominated. There was a free and open debate on all manner of subjects, the leading thinkers of the country addressed the student community and there were cultural programmes involving famous people. We listened to renowned singers, watched important plays and heard talks by remarkable intellectuals. Even the student elections required candidates to participate in an open debate so that the student community could gauge their minds. We forged friendships with our teachers; friendships that were as close as family ties. The students and teachers lived in the same area, so whenever a student faced any problem, he/she would go over to a teacher's home and the teacher would offer them advice and help.

What I liked about JNU was that none of the students had a car or a jeep. Most used bicycles or motorcycles to get around. Clothes were informal—jeans or khadi kurta-pyjamas. Another speciality of JNU was that there were discussions on international issues often and posters were put up and rallies held in support of or against events across the globe. The focus was not just on the country but on the world, so the outlook and sensibility of the students were international.

The university campus, sprawled across a segment of the Aravalli hills, was of modernist design and construction was still on when we got admission. The hostels were ready but the teaching took place in the old building and the compound below, which had been built to train central government staff. The new wing, where our hostels were, did not have a library; that was still on the ground floor and so every day, we made several trips up and down. There was a bus service between these two locations but there was a shortcut down the wooded hill which we used. The architecture of the bhavans was also different. It offered a glimpse of what Nalanda University must have been like at the peak of its existence. The buildings were made of exposed brick with no visible sign of cement or any other adhesive. Every room had a balcony which gave the students an indoor-outdoor feeling. There was a lot of space in the form of maidans between the hostels. Trees dotted the slopes with shrubs planted among them. As far as possible the natural topography of the landscape had been respected.

The style of teaching at JNU was also different. Many centres had been integrated into schools; and even in these centres, subjects were clubbed together to form integrated courses. I was at the Centre for Regional Studies which was part of the School of Social Sciences where I received a post-graduate degree in geography. But it was not just classical geography that was taught there. We also had to study history, political science, sociology, planning and statistics, among others. Marking was not based on a final examination but on an aggregate score. There were research papers to be written. One had to participate in seminars and there were interviews as well. There were open-book examinations too. All this was totally new. In the middle of an exam, we would often take a break, go out for tea and a snack, and then return to write some more. The teachers would take several hours to prepare a one-hour lecture. Students would often visit them in their quarters to discuss research projects. This made students and teachers feel as if they belonged to one family.

There was a traditional belief prevalent among us that if you wanted to succeed at education and in life as well, you could not waste time falling in love. JNU dispelled these notions. There was an atmosphere of freedom at the university but the students behaved in a mature manner. In comparison to most other universities, there was much more mixing between the male and female students.

The girls would often be at the boys' hostel until late at night; they would be studying together and no one remarked on it. Thanks to spending a lot of time together—studying, roaming about, in class or in the library—students got to know each other very well. Friendships often blossomed into love and then, love marriages, which was nothing new. Many of these were inter-religious or inter-caste marriages.

At that time, it was thought to be a courageous, if not historic, step for a Bihari woman to be studying at JNU. The majority of those who sent their daughters to college preferred to keep them close. If they sent them away, it was to traditional universities. And this was JNU! Nevertheless,

Poornima took admission here. The hostels in JNU were named after rivers. I was in Kaveri; she was in Jhelum. Sometimes she would get upset with me. When I wanted to make up, I would take a mutual friend with me. I knew that she would not open the door to her room if she heard my voice so I would ask the friend to call out to her from outside the hostel. Poornima would step out on to the balcony. She would see me with the friend and even if she wanted to, she would not be able to hold on to her anger. We had our ups and downs as any relationship does.

The students at JNU all wore jeans and khadi kurtas. We were not interested in fashion. Wearing our khadi kurtas, we would lie on the floor of the library, reading our books. Books would also form our pillows at times. The library was well-stocked. There was no shortage of books and journals. The library canteen served cheap tea and snacks. Outside of class, we spent most of our time in the library. After dinner at the mess, we would repair to the library, returning to our rooms only at 1 a.m. Because the majority of the courses were post-graduate degrees, the average age of the students was somewhat higher than at other universities. And so, the students were also more mature.

The atmosphere at JNU was very different from that of other universities. There were many students from villages, small towns and middle-class families since these factors were also taken into consideration in the selection process. The other good thing about the university was that there were students from all over the country. The number of students from West Bengal, Bihar and Orissa was larger than expected. Perhaps this was because the standard of education in these States was excellent.

Since students and teachers shared a good relationship, teachers knew their students personally and tried to help with their problems. The emphasis was on research, new ways of thinking and good presentation. The problems of the State and those of the world came up for discussion. Protests were often organized and important public figures came and spoke to the student community.

I scored the highest marks in my department and was selected for an MPhil. I was also getting a scholarship from the University Grants Commission (UGC) which, at that time, was sufficient to cover my expenses.

The language of communication between the students from different States was English. This meant that the students from Bihar and Orissa had to learn English too. We also grew familiar with each other's cultures and languages and began to participate in each other's festivals. Some of the dhabas (eateries) at JNU were open through the night. Many students would meet at the dhabas to talk about their subjects while eating a snack or drinking a cup of tea. We generally got up late in the mornings and so I left my toothbrush and toothpaste in the department. I would pick up a packed breakfast and eat it after brushing my teeth and freshening up. There are many different things that Biharis like to eat. Most of the university workers would bring rotis from home and order a curry or rajma or moong dal to eat with it—I found this a little odd. In front of my centre there was a south Indian dhaba where I developed the habit of eating vadas with coconut chutney. Across the dhaba was a paan shop which I patronized.

The geography syllabus required us to study a particular

State. In our year, the State chosen was Ladakh. Initially it was difficult for Indians to visit Ladakh. We too had to get permission from the local administration. Since it becomes very cold in Ladakh, we had to undertake a great deal of preparation before going there.

The doctors advised us to carry brandy with us. When the temperature fell, they recommended a rubdown with brandy; it could also be drunk with water. There was a big army base at Kargil. One day, two or three of us boys were walking past the camp, talking in Bhojpuri when a couple of sentries stopped us. They were delighted to hear their language since they were from Bihar. They invited us to dinner at the camp. We ate with them and were forced to drink rum. After we left Kargil, we had to live in tents in many places. Most of the trekking happened between 5 a.m. and 10 a.m. when the snow was firm. After 10 a.m., it began to melt, making trekking difficult. Our tents and luggage were loaded on ponies. As the leader of the group, choosing the trail was my responsibility. We often had to find ways to cross the small streams we encountered. Where the flow was not deep, we could cross with the help of ropes. Crossing a stream could leave your feet frozen and they had to be massaged with brandy.

We were trekking through what was then unmapped territory in Ladakh. There were very few trees or even shrubs. In a sense, it was a frozen desert. We camped wherever we could find fresh water, generally at the base of small glaciers. As we were at a very high elevation, oxygen was scarce and breathing became difficult. When we tried to make khichdi, the rice would melt into the water while the dal remained resolutely hard.

Ladakh has two communities: the Buddhists and the Muslims. The Buddhists had a tradition by which the firstborn boy would not marry and would become a monk. The Muslims had a tradition that a woman would marry several men from the same family as there was a shortage of women. The Buddhists and the Muslims lived side-by-side in the same villages in complete harmony. Their staple was barley from which they made flour and which they fermented for chhang, the local tipple. They kept yaks for milk and butter. During the summer, the yaks were taken up to the high meadows and in the winter, they were brought down to the plains. They ate goat meat and chickens were also available. They needed very little from the outside world except for salt, sugar and kerosene. Most of them had never left Ladakh.

The cold was so intense that the exposed parts of our faces turned dark. This was because of the sunlight reflected off the snow. We bought a goat along the way and ate half of it. The other half, we slung up on the branches of a tree. The locals told us we would be able to eat it on the way back. Here, nature does the work of a refrigerator. The people here were not very familiar with money. When we bought chicken, they wanted the big-sized notes from our purses. Even the coins were accepted on the basis of their weight. This was because that area of Ladakh had just been opened up.

Once, as we were trekking, a boulder slipped and the water which had accumulated behind it rushed forth in a torrent. We barely got away with our lives.

Our trek took us from Kargil to Padam. At around

eight o'clock, when we were nearing Padam, we saw a Sardar ji approaching us. He was alone and carrying a bag. We were quite surprised to see him there. When we talked to him, he said that the area had recently been opened up to the public. Ergo the public would need some place to eat. He was planning to open a dhaba there. We began to understand why you will meet a Sardar ji wherever you go in India or across the world.

Padam was a big village. It had electricity for a few hours thanks to a generator. When we reached, we heard that a wedding was to take place that day. We were invited to the festivities and somehow managed to make it to our destination; the snow had melted in many places. Upon entering the house, we found the young woman who was to be married seated by the side of a huge pot, surrounded by her relatives. Everyone had a small brass tumbler in hand. A huge hunk of mutton which was suspended from the ceiling was being cooked by the smoke rising from a fire underneath. We were each given a piece of meat and a brass tumbler of chhang from the pot. The girls who did not drink were seated next to the boys and girls who did. This was because there was a tradition that when the young bride came and stood before anyone, their glass had to be empty. She would then fill the glass with chhang from the pot. To not empty one's glass would be to disrespect the bride. In a few hours we were all very drunk. Late in the night, we bade farewell to our hosts and somehow made our way back to our tents.

When we began trekking the next morning, we swaddled ourselves in warm clothes—sweater, coat, muffler and the like. On our feet, warm socks and shoes. But after walking a while, we would begin to feel hot and take off our clothes. Perhaps our bodies were getting used to the cold. This month-long expedition was an eye-opener for me. It was also when I began drinking alcohol.

I was always something of a teacher's pet and there were some teachers who left a deep impression on me. One of them was Joseph E. Schwartzberg. I was given the opportunity to work with him for six months in JNU. He was one of the leading geographers of the United States who had come to India for a year. I learned from him how difficult and time-consuming research can be. In thirty years of his academic career, he had only published six papers and had created a historic atlas of South Asia. This had taken him seventeen years but it was seen as one of the crowning achievements of his career and one of the greatest achievements in his sphere of endeavour. His research on the castes of India left me amazed. I found that I had much to learn from this North American about India, despite being an Indian myself.

I went with him on his research tours too. He did not like armchair research and would come with us, his research assistants, on field trips even for routine tasks such as data collection. The other professor I was influenced by was Aijaz Ahmed, who was the head of the department of my subject. He was a model of simplicity and had dedicated his entire life to the study of geography. I was his favourite student that year and our relationship became familial. He wanted me to do a PhD in social geography. This was a relatively new field of research and so there was great scope as very little work had been done. He gave me a new perspective with which to view social problems.

There was a rule in the university that if a student scored an A grade (75 per cent), he/she did not have to sit for an examination to register for a PhD. There was only an interview. I got an A grade. My PhD guide was Professor Aijaz Ahmed. He was an expert in social geography. When I appeared for the interview, I only had to announce the topic of my thesis and my guide said that he was willing to take me on. He added that if the interview committee had any further questions, they could put them to him. That brought the interview to an end and I was registered for a PhD.

My guide had selected a topic that made it easy for me to become a lecturer at JNU. He wanted me to continue teaching at JNU and conduct research in social geography. But like other students, I was also looking for a job. I appeared for two bank examinations for the post of Probationary Officer and failed both. I began to study for my UPSC examination.

The majority of JNU students would appear for the competitive examinations after finishing their MA course. I also sat for the UPSC examination. When the results of the preliminary IAS examinations were published in the newspapers, my roll number was not among the successful candidates. Because the other students knew me as a bright student, they assumed that I had passed the examinations. From the morning, congratulations began to pour in. I did nothing to dispel the notion and assuming that I had not passed, I applied for my MPhil research.

A month later, I was eating paan at the university gate

when I was suddenly struck by the desire to board a bus. It was a 623 that went via Shahjahan Road past the UPSC building. I hopped on the bus and when it was passing by the UPSC building, I found myself getting off there. I went into the reception area. On the wall in front of the reception desk, the results were put up. Some of the sheets were torn and some were unclear so I went to the receptionist and said that I should like to check the results. She asked for the roll numbers and I gave her three roll numbers, one of which was mine. She looked them up and said, 'Give me mithai (sweets). All three have passed.'

I said, 'Check again carefully. Two will have passed and one failed.'

She showed me the register and indeed, I had passed! Looking at the register it became clear to me that for some reason the successful candidates with roll numbers between 65,000 and 65,100 had not appeared in the papers. This whole episode had a touch of magic about it. Since I found out that I had got through late, I had only half the time to prepare. Anyway, I returned to the hostel and plunged into preparation for the main examination.

I passed the main examination, qualifying for the interview round. The interview was a bit odd. The chairperson of the committee said that she had been to Bihar and had been given thekua (a sweet made of deep-fried wheat flour and jaggery) to eat which she had found difficult to chew. I explained that this was the prasad offered in Bihar at the time of chhat parva and that is how it is eaten. It is made, I assured her, of various healthy ingredients and so is beneficial to the body. The second and third questions also produced much discussion. This did not seem to be going well and I was not sure of getting through. But when the results were declared, I found that I had scored high marks at the interview and had been given the Bihar cadre as well. This was in 1981 and I was around twenty-three years old then.

I was the first student of my centre to get into the IAS but I was finding it difficult to talk about that to my guide. I would be leaving academics forever and I thought this would not go down well with him. In a great stew of apprehension, I met Professor Aijaz Ahmed's wife and shared the whole story with her. I also told her that I should like to take the family out to dinner. His wife asked me to make the arrangements and promised that they would come. Through the meal, I talked only to Professor Ahmed's wife and his daughter. For his part, Aijaz Sahab said nothing to me but when we returned to his quarters on the JNU campus, he said that the study of geography would stand me in good stead in my new career and gave me his blessings.

I left JNU for Mussoorie. Our training took place in the Lal Bahadur Shastri Administrative Academy. This was in 1981. Mussoorie, tucked away in the heart of nature, is an important tourist destination. It was located earlier in Uttar Pradesh but it is in Uttarakhand today. The views from Mussoorie of the Himalayas and the Doon Ghats are breathtaking as they encompass the ice-covered slopes of the mountains. Mussoorie is also the gateway of Gangotri.

By the way, here is an interesting incident which might illustrate how joining the IAS means the formation of a line of hopeful fathers-in-law at one's door. When the IAS results were declared, I was in JNU. It was a sweltering evening. I was in my hostel room, clad only in a towel. There was a knock on the door. I thought it was a friend and asked him to come in. But it was a stranger. He introduced himself as a coal magnate from Dhanbad.

I said, 'Let me get dressed. Why don't you wait for me at the dhaba?'

At the dhaba, I ordered tea.

The coal magnate came straight to the point, 'How much do you weigh? We will give you your weight in gold.'

I got it. The man was shopping for a son-in-law. Bihar has a sauraat sabha (husband fair) in Mithilaanchal district. I paid for his tea and said goodbye to him.

Each year, 1 September marks the beginning of the training programme of the various arms of the services. After three months, everyone else goes off to their respective training centres; but the IAS entrants remain for the next nine months. There is an army attachment, a tribal attachment, an industrial attachment and a field attachment. It is a two-year-long probation period and a course high on elitism. There was a dress code for dinner, for class and for public events. It was a little like the army and so it was rather difficult for the likes of us.

P.S. Appu, the then director, was a progressive and open-minded person. He was from the Bihar cadre, from the 1951 batch. He had been the Chief Secretary under Chief Minister Karpuri Thakur. When he became the head, he shifted the emphasis from protocol and etiquette to character formation and values. He announced that there would be no dress code from then on. A simple jacket would suffice. We probationers were delighted.

For the field attachment, we had to make a trip to Chamoli—a beautiful town surrounded by mountains, on the road to Badrinath on the banks of the Alaknanda River. On the one hand, there is the tranquillity of religious places and on the other, the scenic attractions of lakes, streams and rivers.

Chamoli teams began to be formed. The batch was divided into four or five groups. I was made the leader of one of the groups. One of our batchmates was a rather arrogant fellow from the Union Territory cadre. He was a resident of Aurangabad, Bihar. Before joining the IAS, he had worked in the Indian Foreign Service (IFS) for a couple of years. He had travelled a bit but was still a loud-mouthed boor. He did not try any of this with me however. Coincidentally, he was assigned to my team. When he heard this, he had himself reassigned. I felt that it was for the best. Renu Singh, UP cadre, was his team leader.

We took turns; when one team returned from Chamoli, the next one set off. I was completely focused on my team to the exclusion of all else. My team and I arrived in Chamoli by bus. We went to the temple first and then roamed around in the village. They have a local liquor brewed from fruit. The bus driver was a habitué who drank a lot of it. I only had a couple of pegs.

Our team went back. Renu Singh's team was up next. Renu asked where they should go first. I said that they should visit the temple. She wanted to go there too. By this time, the arrogant young man had already drunk a lot. One of his friends had challenged him to drink more than the driver and so he was out of control. He did not want to visit the temple. He said, 'Forget it, let's just go to the village.' He ordered the driver to go straight to the village. There were some south Indian probationers in his team who were shocked to see the way he was behaving. One of his friends told him that Renu had directed the bus to head to the temple first. That was it. The agitated probationer pulled out a pistol and headed towards Renu's room. It was night and he was not in his senses. He began to hammer on her door with the pistol. The news reached the District Superintendent of Police, Chamoli. The District Magistrate ordered his team and him to go back to Mussoorie. Appu Sahab had heard of the whole incident. As they neared Mussoorie, the arrogant young man fell at the feet of his team mates, apologizing to all of them. Appu Sahab was a stickler for discipline. He wrote to the Central administration and had the probationer terminated. At that time, Giani Zail Singh was Home Minister and Indira Gandhi was Prime Minister.

We had just dressed for dinner and stepped out of our rooms when we heard the news that the probationer had been terminated. He was boorish and we had not liked him but the news left us a bit shaken. Every evening, we used to watch a film at Mussoorie. That evening, we didn't watch one. We thought that the termination might have been a terrible blow to the probationer. We feared he might commit suicide in despair. Some of us decided to keep a watch on him all night. We posted a helper from the hostel in front of his window to watch over him. But sleep eluded me too. When I went to check on him at around 3 a.m., the helper said that he had had a drink and was fast asleep. Obviously, I had wasted my concern!

One of the rules was that every morning we had to do either a bout of physical training or yoga. Then we had class which went on up to lunch. Some classes would spill over into the afternoon. At 4 p.m., I would be on the playing fields, working up a good sweat at volleyball or badminton. Appu Sahab often joined us. During the orientation programme, two probationers shared a hostel room. My room partner was an IPS officer from the Haryana cadre. He was an extremely disciplined person. He would get up early in the morning while I was a late riser. I would sleep in my PT uniform and tell Pandey ji to wake me up twenty minutes before the appointed time.

One day, so much snow fell that the entire city of Mussoorie lost its electric supply. We had to melt snow for drinking water. The situation was so bad that we were all granted leave. I came to Delhi. Poornima was studying at JNU at the time. We kept meeting through the training period. Once, she had even come to Mussoorie to meet me. She was wearing jeans that day. I was going to eat paan with my friends after lunch and we walked right past her without realizing it. Only when she called out did I stop. When I start doing something, I get so engrossed that the observer might think I am ignoring him/her but this is not deliberate.

Our friendship turned into love. We wanted to get married. Now the question was which one of us would break the news to her parents. Poornima's father was a highly principled man, an old-style communist. Poornima was not sure that she could confront her parents. So I went to meet her family in Kankhal Bagh, where they lived, to ask for her hand in marriage. Our marriage was fixed and we got married in 1981. It was a marriage based on ideals with no exchange of money. Although I was marrying someone from my own caste, it was a love marriage.

4

The Journey from One District to Another

Next came our field posting. The main idea of the field posting is that the officers of the IAS should get to study a district in detail: its geography, its administrative structures and major occupations. They should learn to find solutions to unexpected problems and get a chance to put government schemes into operation on the ground. My first field posting was in Purnia in 1982–83. After that, I was posted to Hazaribagh, Gopalganj, Vaishali, Dhumka, Purnia, Tremandal (Muzzafarpur) and Tirkut. Each has a story of its own.

Purnia was considered a poor and backward district. Most of the houses were shacks with tin roofs; cement houses were few and far between. As far as the eye could see, there were fields stretching ahead, intercut by streams. I had a great experience at Purnia. The internship period is really dependent on your relationship with the District Collector. Fortunately, I had a friendly relationship with him. Almost every night, we had dinner together. But when I was moved to various sections of the Collectorate, most officers did not even recognize me. They believed that if I had been posted to the Treasury, I should stay at the Treasury and see how bills were passed in reality. This meant that I learned most of the work through the good offices of the assistants. There were no arrangements in place to help me to learn the work though this was perhaps all for the best.

Apart from the training, I also indulged my interests. Not far from Purnia was the Khaja Palace of the Maharaja of Darbhanga. Next to it, a huge lake called Khaja Lake had been dug. I began the work of restoring the palace and cleaning up the lake. It was teeming with fish, some of them weighing as much as thirty to forty kilos and people fished using spears. There was a lot of land around the lake where trees had been planted. The kothi (mansion) which stood on a mound near the lake was turned into a four-room rest house.

It was decided that the renovated Khaja Kothi and boating on the Khaja Lake would be inaugurated by His Excellency the Governor. Khaja Kothi was about one-and-a-half kilometres from the road. The Road Construction department said it was impossible to build a road connecting it in such a short span of time. I said, 'Nothing is impossible. If it has to be built, it has to be built.' Working day and night, we got the road built. The Governor, Mr A.R. Kidwai, arrived for the inauguration and spent a night at the guest house.

At one point, the Chief Minister had a programme in Purnia. News spread that the executive engineers of the four major departments were being transferred. I found this surprising because two of them had only just arrived and were doing good work. When I went to meet the Chief Officer about this, he said, 'No such thing will happen. Wait and watch.' It turned out that some local politician had spread the rumour about these transfers and had taken fifty thousand rupees from each of the engineers. He then told them that he had prevented the transfers from happening.

I found out that the money had been used partly for bringing in people to attend the CM's programme and the rest had been pocketed by the leader.

When the CM was to arrive at Purnia, I was put on duty at the aerodrome so that I might learn the protocols of such a reception. When the government plane carrying the CM landed, the door opened and first, a lady legislator stepped out; she was followed by a minority community legislator. After that came a legislator from the Scheduled Tribes and then the Honourable CM. He was greeted according to protocol. Then the local leaders were introduced. One of them performed a full prostration, a sashtang namaskar, at the CM's feet. This was the man who had hoodwinked the engineers and brought disrepute to the party's name. A case had been registered against him.

The CM looked furious and he said, 'I know you will get rid of him quickly.'

Right after that, another man performed the same prostration, claiming that the first politician was as pure as the driven snow and this was all the doing of his enemies. People were slinging mud simply to get rid of him; he was actually the CM's most faithful ally. To which the CM replied, again in anger, that he knew all about these conspiracies. As long as he was around, no one would be able to unseat the leader and it was because of such leaders that the party was surging ahead.

These two incidents, separated by a matter of minutes, was a great learning for me. It was also very surprising. I had never seen anything like it, not even in a film.

An IAS probationer must also work as a Block Development Officer or a Circle Officer. I was sent to the east block of Purnia city. There were many incidents of arson there. A man came to meet me saying that he was very poor and his crop had been destroyed by fire. On inquiring, I discovered that he owned forty bighas of land. It seemed quite surprising that someone should own forty bighas and still claim poverty. Where I come from, five bighas is considered a pretty substantial land holding from which a good crop can be expected. His land was situated near a river. The soil was rich and fertile. The fields were covered by Kans grass and this was what had burned.

It was then that I remembered a tale Renu ji had told me. In olden times, Purnia was famous for its rose market. This was held in a huge maidan where an annual fair happened. Slowly, the merchants began to encroach on the maidan, building cement houses for themselves. My office had a huge file on the encroachments. It became clear that despite many notices, these structures had not been demolished. I met the Circle Officer who said that if I were bent on clearing away these buildings, I could but I would only be there for a short while these encroachments had happened over decades. Anyway, I formulated a plan for clearing them, hired a hundred labourers and two road-rollers and arrived on the spot. The residents did not seem particularly worried which filled me with a mixture of surprise and anger.

Then the local MLA turned up. His name was Ajit Sarkar. He said that these homes were very old and a Zone Officer like myself had no business destroying them. I said that I was going to do it anyway. He lay down on the street and said that I would have to run the road-rollers over him. I had a jeep assigned to me. I told the policemen with me to pick Sarkar up and put him in the jeep and take him to the police station. Then I began the work of demolition. The people who were in the houses were moved out. For most of the owners, this was a second or even a third house. They were allowed to remove their goods before the houses came down.

The matter went to the Patna High Court which passed a stay order, halting the work. By this time, 90 per cent of the construction had already been demolished, and on the pretext of clearing the debris, the other 10 per cent was also razed.

Then, a newspaper of the time, *Ravivar*, carried a story saying that the courts had been superseded by a bureaucrat. The State government ordered my transfer. I had just a month left of training. The Circle Officer requested a clarification in the matter of the transfer of an officer in training and my last month ended in this exchange.

The matter caused much comment in the Bihar Vidhan Sabha. The Honourable Member raised a motion of privilege against me. A committee of three members was instituted. They conducted their inquiry for a year by which time the Vidhan Sabha's term ended. But just before that, the Speaker, Radhanandan Jha, asked for the file and wrote on it that he was satisfied I had acted within the ambit of my duties and that there was no question of a breach of privilege.

When I was in charge of Nazarat district in Bihar, news of a raise in pay came, and the governor Mr A.R. Kidwai had gone to Kishanganj. The food he had been served there included a chicken curry that cost one-hundred-and-seventy-five rupees per plate. Perhaps it is possible to understand what one-hundred-and-seventy-five rupees meant if you consider that my salary at that time was one thousand two hundred rupees per month. To investigate the matter, I went with the Additional Collector to the dak bangla in Kishanganj. In those days, whenever I travelled, I would carry my food in a tiffin. I would drink the local water. I called the restaurateur and the Additional Collector asked him why the chicken curry was so expensive. He replied that it was made of desi chicken cooked with dry fruit. The Additional Collector told him to serve us two plates of the same curry. I got angry for we had come to investigate the price of the curry; how could we possibly be eating it? His contention was that we could only know whether such a curry could be worth the price by trying it out ourselves. Eventually, two plates of the chicken curry were served and the Additional Collector opined that the price was reasonable since the curry had indeed been cooked with pistachios and almonds. When we returned to Purnia, I explained the matter to the Circle Officer.

Another significant incident occurred in Purnia—it was a long-standing case of encroachment at a haat. A haat is defined as a temporary market where stalls are allowed to be erected for the day and must be removed once the market is done. No permanent structures may be built there. I went to Sairaat with the Additional Collector to conduct an investigation.

Along one edge of the maidan there was the revenue office, two rooms which were meant for the revenue officers to stay. When we arrived, the air was redolent with the aromas of cooking. Sweetmeats were being prepared and puris and kachoris were being fried. Fish too was being fried and mutton sizzling away. I asked what was going on and was told that the food was being prepared for the officers who were on their way. I told the Additional Commissioner that I would eat nothing of this and would content myself with the food I had brought with me. The Additional Commissioner sighed and said that this was the case with the young people who had just joined the service. They were always getting angry but this was only because of a lack of experience.

Anyway, I left with a revenue worker to investigate the illegal cement structures that had come up. We found thirty-two of them. The sellers had built homes and were running permanent shops from them. With the help of the revenue worker, I made a thorough inspection and prepared a detailed report of the encroachment. When we returned to the revenue office, the honourable Additional Commissioner was finishing lunch. A silver tray filled with the choicest sweetmeats awaited him. I explained the situation saying that we had to demolish these structures and also start other legal proceedings against them. The Additional Commissioner called all thirty-two encroachers and when they had congregated, he pulled them up and told the revenue worker to initiate cases against all of them. I found it surprising that he could eat the good food they had prepared for him and then abuse them roundly. The report he sent to the Circle Officer was exactly the one I had prepared. The Additional Commissioner explained that making tough decisions was the responsibility of the government officer but it was equally the responsibility of the sellers to arrange for our hospitality.

During the Second World War, thousands of Indians fled to Burma. In the days of the British Raj many Indians had sought employment or business opportunities in that country. Then Japan attacked Burma, which was also beginning to experience the birth pangs of an independence movement, and the presence of Indians was seen as a symbol of colonialism. Hence, as the intensity of the war increased, there was a wave of reverse migration to India. Many people from Bhojpur in Bihar had gone to Burma and when they returned, they were treated as refugees and relocated in various parts of the country. Some families were placed in Araria in Raniganj district. Each family was given three acres of land by the government. These people still speak Bhojpuri rather than the languages spoken in Araria or in Purnia.

My friend had some good farming land at Araria,

Raniganj. All around his farm there was a settlement of refugees. These were the Bhojpuris who had gone to Burma and returned home. The government had given each family three acres of land fifty years ago. They were an industrious and hard-working lot who would raise three crops of cabbage each year and three crops of corn. They would also sow new and different types of vegetables. They had made decent money on seasonal vegetables. Nepal was close by. Many new varieties of seeds came to Nepal from China and they would buy these too and sow them. Their children were sent to other States to learn new agricultural techniques.

They also grew medicinal herbs. In addition, they reared cows, goats and chickens and so they were quite prosperous. After I went there, a school was opened in the village and contact with Raniganj improved. I would send representatives of the agricultural department to the area so that they could learn something for I too had learned much from these farmers. Without much help from the government, a society can bootstrap itself into relative prosperity. They were a perfect example of this.

The districts of Purnia and Koshy were famous for their bananas. They were a good cash crop for the entire area. Then came a surge in the global demand for corn. The entire district has been completely transformed today. Farming is a hugely profitable enterprise. This change, wrought by corn, happened without government assistance. When people see a demand, they change the pattern of their crops. Corn now fetches higher prices than wheat or rice.

After my probation in Purnia, I was posted to Hazaribagh as Sub-divisional Officer (SDO). Hazaribagh is a district of hills, jungles and Adivasis. I love spending time in the jungle as well as trekking. When the files began to pile up, I would retreat to a forest guest house and work my way through them there. We had jeeps assigned to us. I enjoyed driving into the hilly areas, meeting the Adivasis and understanding their problems. My time at Hazaribagh is entwined with memories of Karpuri Thakur who was the leader of the opposition at that time. The SDO had been assigned a new jeep. I was sent with him to receive Karpuri ji. Ramnika Gupta, the then MLA, tried to incite Karpuri ji by pointing out that I had come to receive him in a jeep rather than a car. Only the District Magistrate had a car in those days.

Karpuri ji's reply made me his slave. He said, 'The SDO has done his best. What more could be expected of him?'

I was impressed by Karpuri ji's simplicity. That day, he returned from a function late in the night. The Circuit House gate was open and so he walked in but the room that was reserved for him was locked. The guard was asleep. Karpuri ji did not think it right to wake the man. He tossed a gamchi (towel) on the dining room table, turned his jhola (bag) into a pillow and went to sleep.

Once, I had gone to examine the construction of homes for Adivasis in Demotand, Hazaribagh. I found that many houses had been built on a maidan but no one was living in them. I called the people who were supposed to live there and talked to them. The elders said that they could not live in houses like these. Their homes were generally built of wood and leaves in which they lived comfortably. They had a belief that if a family had a house that used lime in its construction during the rains, that family would be ostracized. Then the family would have to build a new house and feed the entire community so that it might be reinstated.

The government houses that had been built for them had cement floors and the windows and doors were very large. Following their suggestions, we changed the floors to mud and reduced the sizes of the windows and doors to acceptable standards. Then, they agreed to live in those houses. Once again, it became clear that the government must engage in dialogue with those it seeks to help. Asking a city-based design firm to throw up a standard module and then imposing that on everyone does not work.

When I was SDO at Hazaribagh, Mr K.V. Saksena was posted as Commissioner there. He was well-known for his devotion to the cause of the poor and his opposition to corruption. The homes of the Commissioner and SDO were next to each other. He lived alone and so did I. His office and his quarters were besieged by poor petitioners. I was often summoned to provide solutions so I made it a habit to check in every day at the Commissioner's office and only then go to mine. At the Commissioner's office, there would be at least eight to ten cases which would need resolution. Many of these were crimes against women.

The coal belt in Hazaribagh had a rule that if there was coal on your land, one member of your family would get a job. A large number of non-Biharis had married Adivasi girls although they were already married. In this way, they became a 'member' of that Adivasi family and got a job. Later, when the first wife and children would arrive on the scene, problems would begin. Most of the workers in the coal mines were in the grip of usurious moneylenders. On payday, the agents of these moneylenders would be waiting to collect their 'dues'.

One of the regular complaints I heard was of wife-beating. I would get the police to summon the accused. The harassment laws were not as strict then and the police officers were not impressed and demanded to know what crime the man had committed since they did not see beating one's wife as a criminal offence. They would give the man a stern lecture, whack him a couple of times with a lathi and send him home, hoping that this would be a deterrent. Unfortunately, it often had the reverse effect. The woman would turn up a few days later with a broken limb, saying that her husband had beaten her even more severely. I would have to take the woman to the hospital to get the bone set and a plaster cast put on it.

There was one interesting case where a young woman had a relationship with the owner of a cinema hall who was now refusing to marry her. One night, I invited the Reserve Superintendent over and the two of us drank a couple of pegs and then began the investigation. We called the cinema hall owner over and warned him. We threatened him with jail but he was adamant. He said he was willing to go to prison but he would not marry this woman. It was his contention that she had made similar accusations about other men before.

Some evenings, Saksena Sahab and I would visit the villages of what in bureaucratic parlance are known as aadim jaati (primitive tribes). I would drive the jeep and he would sit by my side. Undeterred by an allergy to dust and a case of chronic asthma, he would wrap a handkerchief over his face and jump into the jeep. Each time we went there, we would load some sick people into the jeep and on our return, get them admitted to hospital. Saksena Sahab spent the majority of his salary on these cases. He asked every one of them whether they had enough money to return home. If they did not, he would give them the money for a bus or rail ticket. If the case occasioned greater sums than he could manage, he would get hold of the Lions or Rotary Club and get the funds from them. The Commissioner and I made the work of the District Officer extremely easy.

Another experience I had was with the animal husbandry schemes. Every mountain dwelling family had two or three goats, four of five chickens, a parrot and some kept a couple of pigs. However, the government scheme mandated twenty nanny-goats and two billy-goats per family. The chicken scheme was for fifty chickens. No one had any experience of dealing with such large numbers nor did they have the ability to do it. I took the decision that we should create units which would have two chickens, two nanny goats, a billy-goat and a parrot. Everyone accepted this scheme willingly.

One day, I had to go to one of the Adivasi villages to resolve a matter of a bank loan default. Someone had taken a loan of five thousand rupees under an animal husbandry scheme. I asked the man where his animals were and why he had not repaid the money. He said that he knew debt was a very bad thing but he had been forced to take the loan and when he received the money, he had kept it with him untouched. He went into his house and pulled out a bundle of notes wrapped in crumpled newspaper. Inside the newspaper was four thousand rupees.

This made it clear that the officer in charge had swallowed a thousand rupees. I instructed the bank representative to receive the four thousand and discharge the debt in its entirety or else I would initiate a case of corruption against the bank. Eventually, the man was declared debt free.

The Commissioner A.C. Suvarno had asked for a report on the success of the bank loan scheme for the low-income group. The report showed that a bank in Ramgarh city had showed very little interest in the scheme. The Honourable Commissioner told me that he was going to Ramgad and would stop at the bank there to investigate the reasons for their lacklustre performance. I suggested that I could handle it but he was adamant. I got into the car and we went to Ramgarh together. There he rebuked the bank manager sternly. The manager assured us that he would address the issue and we would see a marked change within a month. The Commissioner was not appeased. He said, '*Is bank mein taala lagaa denaa chaahiye*' (The doors of this bank should be locked). What I did not know was that his bodyguard had brought along a huge lock with a length of chain. Having said what he had said, the Commissioner proceeded to Dhanbad.

I called the bank manager and told him to get the day's work done as soon as possible because the lock had arrived. And when the employees had all left, we did indeed set a lock upon the doors. The news of this spread across the nation. The bank union immediately requested the Central government to open the bank. Now we had to prove that we had done the right thing in locking the bank's doors and we had to reopen the branch. I went to the Ramgad Camp Office and issued an order under Section 144 of the Indian Penal Code. The story we invented was that this bank had been giving loans to the poor with such enthusiasm that it was being mobbed by thousands of poor villagers. I had begun to fear that the mob might prove uncontrollable and damage the bank property. In order to secure the branch and ensure the safety of its employees, I had had a lock put on the door. After much explaining, so my story went, the crowds had been dispersed with the assurance that their loans would be sanctioned within the month. I gave all this information to the officer who had arrived in Dhanbad. The officer concurred that I had done the right thing in invoking Section 144. He said that he would send the order he had received to reopen the bank branch to my court. I told him that I had acted as the court when I was only a Circle Officer. The Central government could at any point in time remove me from this post.

The bank union wanted me suspended and other actions taken against me. I opened the bank the next day and got the manager's pending applications passed within the week. But the Central government still wanted to move against me. At that time, the Chief Secretary found a beautiful bureaucratic solution to the issue. He got the government to pass an order saying that banks and government officials often found themselves at loggerheads. And so, the State government should take a policy decision that when there was an issue between a Circle Officer and a bank, the solution was to be found by the Commissioner. And if it were an issue between the Commissioner and a bank, then the State government would have jurisdiction. In this manner, I was saved from suspension.

In front of the office of the Circle Officer stood a fine old government building which had been, once upon a time, the office of the Executive Engineer. This building was in the palace area and the State government had the right to assign it for use. One of the audacious Executive Engineers had, at the end of his term, sent in a request to use the building as his residence. Although this had not been approved, he had continued to stay there. This illegal possession had gone on for a long time.

When I devised a plan to end his illegal stay, many people tried to dissuade me saying that he had powerful political protectors and that any such scheme would fail. I sent him a notice requiring him to vacate the premises within a week but this had no effect. The man came to meet me and explained that I was still wet behind the ears and that my career lay ahead of me. He said that taking him on would adversely affect my career. And the Executive Engineer was not going to vacate in any case. I went to the Reserve Superintendent and asked for a large contingent of policemen to go with me. The next day, when we were supposed to get the house vacated, I found that there were no policemen available and the Station Officer, the Inspector and the Deputy Commissioner of Police were not in the station; all of them were out on 'inspection duty'.

At that time, the Circle and District Offices had a panel of peons. I got the Deputy Collector of Nazarat to summon fifty young men who had applied for the post of peon and asked him to organize a hearty meal for them. After they had enjoyed lashings of meat chawal, we went to the house. The fifty peons made short work of emptying the house, and all its contents were dumped outside, on the road. Simultaneously, I moved in the material for my supply office into the building and posted a signboard to that effect on it.

I knew that there would be interference from higher levels and so I made a video of the Supply Office and placed guards around the household goods on the road. I sent the two sons of the encroacher to the police station and asked the police to institute cases against them for interfering with a government officer in the performance of his duties and for encroachment. That night, when the Reserve Deputy Superintendent went to the police station, we found the two young men sitting on the Station Officer's chair and eating ras malai. The other policemen were busy entertaining them. I had the lock-up opened and put them in there. I gave a written report that the Station Officers were conspiring with the accused and that proceedings should be instituted against them.

Late in the night, the Reserve Superintendent visited my house and said that if I were to take action against these officers, there would be a rebellion in the police ranks. My stand was that we should not encourage criminal activities and that action should certainly be taken against them. In the end, they were transferred from their posts, thanks to the intervention of the Circle Officer. The next day, the

High Court at Ranchi issued a stay order. The engineer who had retired came to me with the order and said that my actions had been nullified. I told him to read the order again carefully. If it was a stay order to keep things going as they were then the orders of the court should be followed to the letter. The Supply Office would continue to remain a Supply Office and his household goods would continue to remain on the road. A few days later, the erstwhile illegal occupant collected his belongings and left. In this way, a government building was freed from encroachment.

Hazaribagh had a history of communal tension. Every year, there would be untoward incidents around the time of Durga Puja and Muharram. Most of them happened because of the route. The Hindus wanted to take their processions via Muslim majority areas where they would stop in front of mosques and play loud music so as to disrupt the prayers. The challenge for the administration was to make sure that they passed through these areas at the right time.

In my circle, there was a big incident during the Durga Pooja procession in Badkagaon district. Some of the processions would refuse to follow the prescribed route and wanted to pass through the Muslim-dominated areas. I said that this time, everyone would follow the route and the route given would be the right one. This did occasion some protest. Earlier administrations had bowed to pressure and had allowed processions to pass at will. I called a meeting of the Pooja Committees and announced that this time the processions would go through the established route only. The tradition was that processions from thirty to forty villages would wind their way along established routes and head for a large maidan. There would be a programme that lasted a while and then the idols would be immersed.

I was handling the Hazaribagh processions when news came that Badkagaon was breaking the rules and insisting on passing through Muslim-majority areas. When they were prevented from doing so, they stopped in their tracks and said that they would not proceed. I went to the spot and discussions continued until late in the night. I was convinced that the programme at the big maidan was going to end quite soon but inside information had it that the committee leaders had a plan to attack Muslim-majority areas that night since there would be a huge number of Muslims at the maidan; and after this attack, the Muslims would give up any idea of opposing the processions. Time passed. Dawn was beginning to break. I told the leaders clearly that I would do everything in my power to prevent them from attacking any village.

When they began to move towards the village, I deployed the police force that I had at my disposal and there was a mild lathi charge. In response, the villagers began to shoot at the police. This left the police with no alternative but to retaliate with gunfire. Three people were killed in the melee. It was important to have the corpses removed. The firing had the effect of dispersing the mob who began to return home. After this, we deployed a huge contingent of policemen in the area.

My anger mounted; I wanted to teach them a lesson for their communally-charged behaviour. It was difficult to provide food for all the police personnel who had arrived to maintain the peace. I gave orders that they were to commandeer all the crops, the vegetables, the chickens and the goats of the wealthy people of the area. The poor were to be excused. For the next ten days, the police dined at their expense, taking their grain, vegetables, chickens, goats and milk. When my jeep passed through their villages, people would scuttle into their houses and close the doors.

During training we were told that when a communal incident occurred, we should watch out to see if any damage had been done to life or property. We held meetings in every village to inquire after missing persons. At one place, we heard that a Hindu man had gone to his in-laws' house in the next village.

We began to investigate. During the course of our inquiries, a child who was herding animals told us that there seemed to be something suspicious going on by the banks of the river. Ominously, crows and kites were circling the spot. When we went there, we found a severed arm with a tattoo on it. The tattoo was the name of the missing man. The village next to the spot was a Muslim-majority one.

The next morning at 5 a.m., I reached the village with a contingent of police. The Reserve Superintendent was with me. We had the village surrounded and after searching every house, we gathered all the men between twenty and forty years of age and brought them to the maidan. We began to interrogate them. It was then that I learned the techniques of investigation. They were made to sit in four or five rooms of the school, one man to a room. During the interrogation, the man in Room One was told that a man in the next room had said that he had ordered the murder. In Room Two, the man was told that the man in Room One had said that he provided the weapon with which the murder was committed. In the third room, the man was told that information from the other rooms pointed to him as the murderer. In the fourth, the man was told that his friends in the other rooms had said that he had concealed the body. This sowed the seeds of doubt in their heads and within two hours, we found out who had killed the man, what weapon had been used and who had helped to conceal the body. We also recovered the murder weapon.

When the police were gathering the men in the maidan, some of the men's faces were blood spattered. This was because the police were hitting them with the butts of their rifles as they corralled them into the maidan. This enraged me. I tore the uniform of one of the policemen and said that he would be dismissed from the force. This had the required effect and the rest of the officers brought the men in without recourse to violence.

A certain community leader was behind this incident which took place in the village of Mejudgaon, Badkagaon. Later, he even contested the election from the area. We worked hard against his candidacy and he lost badly. He had thought that having created a situation between Hindus and Muslims, he would have secured the Hindu vote. However, this did not happen.

During the Durga Pooja celebrations in the city of Hazaribagh, another communal clash took place. It was the tradition that idols of the goddess would be immersed in one of the big lakes of the city. Once again, the leaders of the procession refused to follow the prescribed route and took the procession through a Muslim-majority area. When they were stopped by the administration, they abandoned the image of the deity and fled. The challenge was now to complete the procession and the immersion. In order to defuse the communally-charged situation, a peace committee was formed. The committee met in the local police station. There, some of the city's Hindu leaders, among whose number were some anti-social elements, assured us that they would immerse the idol. It was my opinion that the administration should supervise the immersion since communal tensions were already running high.

Anyway, the Circle Officer decided that we should entrust them with the responsibility and allow them to complete the ceremony with the help of the people. The manner in which they did this and the slogans they raised proved offensive to Muslims and the two communities began pelting stones at each other. In the fracas, the image of the goddess also suffered some damage. Rumours spread through the city that there were Hindu-Muslim riots and that people were even killing each other. When this happened, the Hindu leaders and their assistants simply fled from the place, as I suspected they would. I had the police go to their homes and arrest them and lock them up in the police station.

Now the challenge was to quell the rumours, repair the idol and have it immersed. Eventually, a hundred police constables in plain clothes did the honours. Curfew was declared. It was announced that the idol had been immersed and that there had been no riots between Hindus and Muslims. It was also made clear that those who had tried to incite such riots had been arrested. For two days, I stayed up late into the night to ensure that anti-social elements did not come out on to the streets—and that if they did, they were promptly arrested. A great deal of illicit alcohol and illegal arms were recovered from the home of the prominent Hindu leader who had tried to start the riots.

These two incidents of communal violence made things very clear. The first was that one had to deal with these situations quickly and firmly. If on the first day, stern action is taken against two or three ring-leaders, the rest understand that their actions will have consequences regardless of who they are. The second was that a peace committee should be composed of the people who might take part in these incidents rather than the elders of the communities involved.

※

One day, I had travelled to Patna for some work. My in-laws lived in Kankhal and I had gone to visit them. I was eating paan with my brother-in-law at a paan shop when a young man came up to my brother-in-law and said, 'Let's go, I want to celebrate with some sweets. Thanks to "jijaji", everything is going fine.' My brother-in-law asked him what job he was doing. He said that he was in the business of transporting coal from Hazaribagh. He had announced that he had made it known in Hazaribagh that his jijaji (brother-in-law) was the Circle Officer of Hazaribagh and that he was transporting coal in his jijaji's trucks. Using this name meant he was never bothered by the police or by the traffic cops and this helped him save a lot of money. His trucks were never checked either.

I was listening to all this with great interest. The young man said that there was one rogue Traffic Inspector who insisted that whoever the owner was, he would still have to pay. This man used his brain and told the Traffic Inspector, 'Sure, but I have no money on me. You will have to ask the Sub-divisional Officer for the money.' When he turned his vehicle in the direction of the SDO's house, the Traffic Inspector lost his nerve and let him go. The man was obviously relishing his recital of these events without knowing that the SDO whom he claimed to be his brother-in-law was me.

When I returned to Hazaribagh, I made inquiries with the Reserve Superintendent and had the man sent to jail. I also instituted departmental inquiries against those who had been demanding money and had them suspended.

Hazaribagh had a huge Tata coal mine. The coal was of good quality and open cast mining was used which was economical. Some of the Adivasis of Hazaribagh came to the Commissioner, K.V. Saksena, saying that they had lost their land to the mine. The Tatas had paid them compensation but had not employed any of them. I sent a notice to the management. In reply, the management said that this was an old matter and compensation had been paid. Furthermore, at the time of making the payment, none of the recipient families had had an adult member who could be employed. I heard that Russi Modi was coming to Charhi so I decided to go there. I told him about a case. The family had a twenty-year-old son and a sixteen-year-old son. Mr Modi said that he had been given to understand that there was no legal requirement to provide such a job but he added that it was important to do more than the law required. Not only did he give the twenty-year-old a job but he also reserved a job for the sixteen-year-old.

In the course of our conversation, he came to know that I was building a stadium in the city of Hazaribagh. He immediately instructed his technical team to go and see in what way they could help. The next day, the team arrived with all kinds of sophisticated equipment and the work of building the stadium was accelerated. In the few hours that I spent with Mr Russi Modi, I learned a great deal about management techniques.

In 1984, when Prime Minister Indira Gandhi was assassinated by her Sikh bodyguards, the nation was rocked by a series of anti-Sikh riots. There were two regimental offices—of the Sikh Regiment and of the Punjab Regiment—in Ramgarh in the Hazaribagh Circle. The Sikh Regiment was composed of Sikhs only; the Punjab Regiment was a mixed one with non-Sikhs as well. At that time, Ramgarh was part of the Hazaribagh Circle and I would go there for a number of reasons including attending Camp Court. I was also in charge of the Chhavni area and so I would often meet the Commanding Officers of both regiments. There was a big population of Sikhs in Ramgarh which had a close connection with the army regiments stationed there.

One day, when I had gone to have dinner at the home of Brigadier Puri, the Commanding Officer of the Sikh Regiment, I asked him whether the tension in the Sikh community had affected the regiment. He replied that civilians were not thinking straight and that all the jawaans and officers of the Sikh Regiment were like his children.

Still, I thought it wise to tell him about the rumours that were floating about in the Ramgarh bazaar. It was being said that the jawaans of the Sikh Regiment were not getting leave to go home. They were worried about the safety of their families. Even the letters they received were being screened.

Three days later, when I was in Hazaribagh, news arrived at about 9 a.m. from Ramgarh that a large number of the soldiers of the Sikh Regiment had emerged from the barracks and were firing shots in the air. When I made inquiries, the Reserve Officer was in Ranchi where he too had heard about the incident. The Circle Officer had just arrived at his post and had gone to Patna to fetch his luggage. That left me as the highest ranking official in the district. I set out for Ramgarh. The Circle Officer had a jeep assigned for his/her use. I was driving the jeep and the driver was sitting in the backseat. I did not use the red lamp so the vehicle looked like it belonged to a civilian. When I was about fifteen to twenty kilometres away from Ramgarh, I could see dozens of trucks full of Sikh soldiers, headed in the direction of Ramgarh. They were firing into the air and raising slogans like, 'Bhindranwale zindabad!' and 'Indira Gandhi murdabad!' and 'Punjab chalo!' When he took stock of the situation, the driver offered to take over the wheel but I refused.

I drove to Charhi police station, off the main road. When I got in touch with Ramgarh over the wireless, I heard from the Reserve Circle Officer that the jawaans of the Sikh Regiment had murdered Brigadier Puri and had looted the arms depot as well as the canteen. They were coming out on to the roads and hijacking civilian vehicles. At first, they had only focused on trucks but later had commandeered buses and private cars in order to get to Punjab. I also found out that some dharamguru or religious teacher had come to the gurudwara in the area and had incited everyone. He said that women were being raped and men were being killed in huge numbers in Punjab. He told them that it was their duty to arm themselves and go to Punjab to defend their relatives.

When Brigadier Puri had heard about this dharamguru's speech, he told his officers that he would go personally and explain things to the man. 'Some of our boys might have become disturbed,' he said. 'But I will handle it.' When he arrived at the arms store, which was in the process of being looted, the jawaans opened fire and riddled him with bullets. What was really astonishing was that the Punjab Regiment was right next door but showed not the slightest interest in stopping the incident and concentrated on its own safety. The Commanding Officer there had sent his family away with all possible security.

I informed the Bihar Home Ministry in Patna about this and asked for the army to be sent from Patna to stop the riots. A control room was set up in Patna. I got an order from the control room that the people on their way to Punjab on the main roads should be stopped with blasts. I found out from the police that there were ten or twelve constables whose main skills seemed to be the ability to conduct a pooja or cook food, etc. The rest were deputed to other places. During my time at the IAS training period when we had interacted with the army, I had discovered that they had highly modern and sophisticated weapons while our police force had only .303 rifles. The other question was how these roads were to be blown up. I talked to the coal mines in my district and they said that they had an explosives store in Ramgarh. It would take about four to five hours to get the explosives out to blow up the roads.

I explained the situation to Patna and said that it was my opinion that only the army would be able to stop this. The local police would be unable to handle the situation. The Reserve Superintendent from Hazaribagh was on his way from Ranchi to Hazaribagh. I requested him to stop all vehicles coming from Ranchi so that the rest would not be able to get transport from Ramgarh to Punjab. Then I heard that all the vehicles that had set out from Ramgarh had come to the Hazaribagh bus stand and had stopped there. There was a shortage of fuel. Most of the people had drunk a lot of looted alcohol but when they began to get sober, they were all for surrendering to some representative of the administration. They were worried that they might be court martialled and that there would be serious consequences. The problems increased as the buses plying between Bihar and West Bengal, carrying ordinary people who were travelling for one reason or another, could not move.

Thus, vehicles from other States that were stuck in Hazaribagh had to be despatched home and then there were the ones filled with the soldiers of the Sikh Regiment and their officers who wanted to head to Punjab as well. Many travellers had been stuck on the buses for hours and were hungry and thirsty; they wanted water, tea, milk and other supplies. The ones en route to Punjab were also looking for sustenance.

Anticipating this, I headed back to Hazaribagh and made arrangements for food and water to be supplied. With the help of some representatives, we identified the trucks driven by Sikhs. We lined them up and after they were ready, we filled them with the majority of those who had come from different places but were trying to get back to Punjab. Those who had arrived in other vehicles and wanted to continue travelling in them were also flagged off. We got a message from Patna that a huge contingent of soldiers and officers had set out from Danapur. I told the office in Patna that in about two hours, they would pass Danapur, crossing out of Hazaribagh's borders. They would be in the next district and so the army would have to stop them. Although a huge number had already left, a considerable number were still in Hazaribagh and Ramgarh, travelling in small vehicles. They had decided that it would not be advisable to travel by the main roads and had taken to the village roads on their way to Punjab.

At around 4 p.m., I was informed that the army was leaving Danapur but they only could leave in the night and the next morning found them in Barhi, a hundred and ninety-nine kilometres away. The Commanding Officer's vehicle had broken down and the whole caravan had stopped and could not proceed until it could be repaired.

The next morning, the caravan arrived at Hazaribagh. I got a message from Patna asking me to talk to the Commanding Officer, a Major by designation. I was asked to tell him to return to Patna. It transpired that some of the jawans and officers had abandoned the Grand Trunk Road and reached Patna. Now it was feared that they might cause a problem in the city. I told the regiment from Danapur to turn back. I was informed that the army was being sent from Ranchi this time. The convoy's Commanding Officer was in no mood to listen. He said that his orders were to proceed to Ramgarh and that was where he was going to go. I had read that by protocol, the Circle Officer of a district outranks a Major in the district. I told him that he should talk to his superiors who had given me these orders to relay to him. He was forced to turn the convoy back. The next day, I went to Ramgarh. The area around the Sikh Regiment was in bad shape. The necessary arrangements to cremate Brigadier Puri's corpse were being made. The Reserve Officer had also arrived. We had the Brigadier cremated with full honours and after a complete inspection of the arms depot and the canteen, I sent a detailed report to the administration.

What also came to light was that many of those who had looted weapons were still in the Hazaribagh district because of the shortage of vehicles. It was announced via loudspeakers that all such people should surrender with their weapons to the local police station. As a result, a few dozen did come forward to surrender but most of them brought no weapons. They claimed that they had not looted any weapons but the truth emerged later: these weapons had found their way into the hands of anti-social elements. Some of the sainiks even surrendered to the traffic police.

Many of the fugitives were stopped at Banaras by the army. These events had an adverse effect on the cities of Ramgarh and Hazaribagh. The tension between the Hindu and the Sikh communities increased. At night, one side would raise slogans like, 'Jai Bajrangbali' to which the other would respond with 'Bhindranwaale zindabad'. Through the nights, we sent vehicles making announcements asking people to keep the peace. When the homes of the anti-social elements of both communities were searched, many weapons were recovered. We sent all these to jail. The results were immediate; by the next day, normalcy had been restored.

※

After two years at Hazaribagh, I was transferred to Gopalganj. On this occasion, the Commissioner invited me over for dinner. Saksena Sahab usually cooked for himself. The menu was roti, sabzi and dal. When I was about to start, he brought out a small bottle of rum. He was against alcohol but he knew that I indulged.

From Hazaribagh, I went to Gopalganj as Deputy Development Commissioner. When I arrived in Gopalganj, I had two suitcases with me. The quarters of the Deputy Development Commissioner was a bungalow in the high style of the Raj. There were at least thirty-five staff members wandering around the place. Since my wife was still finishing her PhD at JNU, I was going to be living there alone. I chose a room to stay in. I thought that the thirty-five staff members were people who had come to meet me since I had just arrived. But as time passed, I found that their numbers did not decrease so I asked my Personal Assistant who they were and what they did. He explained that there were three members who had telephone duty for eight hours each; two to look after the cow and two for the dogs. There were seven or eight gardeners, two cooks and the rest were servants and security guards.

I explained that I had no cow and no dogs. I asked him to sort out the required number of staff and redeploy the others. The quarters were not the only overstaffed unit. Later, I found out that the Zilla Parishad had three hundred employees, not many of whom were really necessary. After my decision, eight staff members were retained and the others were removed. I heard that after this happened one of those who had been asked to go jumped off a bridge into the river nearby. He was, however, saved from drowning. He was desperate after he had lost his job.

This incident made me realize that sacking people is not the answer. Instead, they would have to be put to work. And so, a meeting was called of all the people who worked for the Zilla Parishad. This included the workers and the officers. I made it clear that I expected to see work for the salaries that were being paid. Gopalganj had several sugar factories that worked for five or six months of the year. Farmers would bring their cane in bullock carts or piled high on tractors. The Zilla Parishad had the right to tax these vehicles but no one had bothered to collect the taxes for years. I assigned many of the workers to collect these taxes. There several old trees along the roads of the district. When these fell after a storm or due to natural causes, the local anti-social elements would use their muscle to buy this valuable wood at low rates. This was stopped and it was decided that when these trees fell, the wood would be brought to the district headquarters where an auction would be announced and it would be sold in the proper manner and at the proper rates.

The Zilla Parishad began to earn a good income on the sale of wood. The rest of the staff was given the task of making an inventory of the assets of the district and numbering the trees on public land. Others were tasked with securing these assets and guarding them.

The Zilla Parishad also owned some prime property in the city of Gopalganj and it was decided to turn this into a shopping complex. A plan was drawn up and published in the newspapers and bids were invited. A considerable sum was earned therefrom and the shopping complex came up. The upper storeys were let out to banks. When the shopkeepers discovered that they had ten-year leases and the shops had not become their private property, they went to court. The courts pointed out that the terms were clearly indicated in the advertisements. The lease documents made provision for the period for which the shopkeepers would have the use of the space. This brought in such a good income that we could pay the monthly wages out of it when funds were delayed.

Gopalganj was also home to the famous Thave temple. Many Gopalganj residents would sport a red thread around their wrists which was considered protection against the ills of the world. The approved style was a motorcycle, a rifle and a red thread around one's wrist. I found that the young men of the area were tall and well-built but they wasted their time hanging out at tea stalls, trying to push through all kinds of shady deals since employment opportunities were few and far between. Some of them were athletes who excelled in volleyball, football and badminton. I met these young men and asked them whether they would work if jobs were to be found. They said that they would. At that time, there was a Rural Development Scheme which offered an initial investment of a lakh for a self-employment project. I offered thirty of these unemployed athletes a lakh each and let them set up small shops on the Zilla Parishad land at the edge of the roads. Of these, twenty shops did exceedingly well and the young men became local role models. These young men, once branded as anti-social, had turned into entrepreneurs and good citizens with a little push in the right direction.

One evening, I invited many of the worthies of the area over to my quarters. During the course of the evening, one of these gentlemen, a prominent businessman, rose hurriedly to his feet, saying that he feared he had forgotten to lock his car. The Police Superintendent told him that he need not worry; most of the anti-social elements were now working for the Zilla Parishad and so there was little chance of the vehicle being stolen.

A little before I was posted to Gopalganj, the District Officer there had been murdered. This murder had been ordered by a religious leader. The situation in the district was tense. I met with the Police Superintendent and told him that any development work could be started only when the rule of law had been established. Simultaneously, we would have to set the youth to work and give them spaces to channel their youthful energy into sporting activities.

At the same time, we would have to take stern action against the criminal elements in society.

There was a stadium behind my quarters called the Minz Football Stadium. Since there were no stands, not many fans could enjoy the games there. I decided that we should build galleries on all four sides of the stadium and even got the money sanctioned. We needed empty space to build these galleries. I sent a proposal to the government, suggesting that land be taken from the surrounding government buildings for the construction of these galleries. When no reply was forthcoming for a long time, I ordered that the construction should begin anyway. The galleries came up and when they began to be talked about, I was asked to explain how I had built these without the go-ahead from the government. In my reply, I said that the government could send anyone they wanted to inspect the galleries and to check that the money had actually been used in their construction. And the matter ended there.

At one point in time, I was the Returning Officer for the Zilla Parishad. Nominations could be filed up to 11 p.m. Two minutes before the proverbial eleventh hour, a man turned up clutching two pieces of papers in his hands. He handed me one and proceeded to stuff the other into his mouth and eat it. When I announced that only one nomination had been received and read out the name, the people who had gathered there pounced on the man and began to thrash him soundly. I was told that they had all agreed unanimously to nominate one of their number and had given this man the job of filing the nomination papers. And he had eaten that piece of paper and substituted his own name.

The police were called in and everyone was sent off. Later, the man was elected unopposed.

Once, while I was the Deputy Development

Commissioner, I was also the District Officer (in-charge). The Civil Surgeon of the area stormed into my office in a temper. I knew that he had been transferred out of Gopalganj. He had requested to be transferred at his old salary but the person in charge of giving him the certificate stating his old salary wanted a bribe of a hundred rupees to do so. I called the man to my office and asked him if this was true. He said it was. I was outraged and said that there would be an investigation of corruption against him. He said he would willingly face it but pointed out that the Civil Surgeon should also be investigated. The doctor was in the habit of conducting private practice even at the hospital. The accused had taken his son there and the doctor had charged him a hundred rupees. I pointed out that two wrongs did not make a right. However, no action was taken against the accused and the Civil Surgeon got his salary certificate and moved on to his next post.

When I was transferred to Vaishali as District Officer, it was known as a 'Red District'. This was because the DM, the SP and the SDO were all alumni of JNU. Their wives were also alumnae of the university. Rituraj, the Police Superintendent, had married a woman from south India and Tripurari Sharan's wife was from another caste.

It was the time of the Lok Sabha elections. My district included the whole of the Hajipur constituency and two Lok Sabha seats of the Vaishali constituency. I was the District Returning Officer for Hajipur, the District Officer for Vaishali, and the Returning Officer for Muzaffarpur. The Chief Minister's wife, Mrs Kishori Sinha, was contesting from Vaishali and Ram Vilas Paswan was contesting from Hajipur which he won with a record margin of five lakh votes. He also broke the world record for the number of votes polled. In those days, the Election Commission reposed its entire faith in its District Returning Officers. There were election supervisors but they did not interfere in the workings of the election as they do nowadays. After the counting had ended, it seemed that some of the constituencies had recorded cent per cent voting.

The Election Supervisor asked me how many constituencies had sufficient ballot papers to allow for cent per cent voting. I said that we had the capacity to allow for three such constituencies. The Election Supervisor then announced that there were three constituencies that had recorded cent per cent voting. When the count was coming to an end, it was discovered that 4,99,000 votes had gone to Ram Vilas Paswan. His team was eager for that number to cross 5 lakhs. His rival's deposit had been forfeited. I advised Ram Vilas Paswan not to get obsessed by the 5-lakh figure and told him that a victory procession would not be allowed. I did not want any law-and-order problem. He agreed. I sent his opponent home in my own car when the election results were announced and Paswan was elected from the Hajipur constituency to the Lok Sabha. The next day, when the booth-by-booth report was being prepared, it was discovered that the votes cast in favour of Paswan had not been counted in the Rajgopur area. The Election Officer said that the results had already been declared and the certificate had been sent to Paswan and so the uncounted votes should simply be forgotten/erased from the record or problems might arise. However, I was not happy. I ordered a booth-by-booth recount and Paswan won by more than 5 lakhs. I sent word of this to the Election Commission and to the Election Commissioner as it was a bona fide mistake and there was no change in the results. The new tally was easily accepted by the Election Commission. I called Paswan and informed him that he had crossed 5 lakhs anyway.

I had conducted the preparations for the election in a scientific manner and so every task had been completed two days before the election. I told my team that leaving things for the last minute was the sign of a weak team. We also counted the votes in record time for Bihar (under twelve hours) and this was before computers and Electronic Voting Machines (EVMs) were around. We were counting actual ballot paper. This was possible because we had used only bank workers for the counting. They came from Patna. I arranged buses and brought them to Hajipur in the mornings and they would finish the counting by 7 in the evenings.

It was said that the Vaishali Lok Sabha seat would witness a titanic battle between the two candidates. The Muzaffarpur Commissioner and the Deputy Inspector General were both confident that the CM's wife would coast to an easy victory. I, on the other hand, would only say that we were going to witness a tough fight. Ms Kishori Sinha found it surprising that I should say this when everyone else was predicting a victory for her.

Many people would come down from Patna to Hajipur on election inspection duty. They would stop by at my office for a cup of tea. They would say that they had gone over the entire area and everything was fine when this was far from the truth. I knew for a fact that some people had come from Patna as well as from places outside it carrying weapons. One such group was drunk in broad daylight and perhaps, because of this, their car got stuck at a railway crossing. Seeing their predicament, some children from a nearby village came running to help them. The intoxicated men thought that they were under attack, stepped out of the car and fled. When I arrived, the children had pushed the car off the tracks and into the water that had accumulated by the side of the road. When the car was extricated from there, many weapons were found inside it. On inquiry, it was discovered that the men were outsiders who had come to the area to cause mischief.

We heard that there was a similar group in Lalganj. When a raid was mounted, ten or twelve men were found, all rather drunk and armed to the teeth, obviously intent on planning a disruption in the district. A unit of the Central Reserve Police Force surrounded them and many country-made revolvers, bombs, hand grenades and money were confiscated.

The then Prime Minister Rajiv Gandhi came to Vaishali to campaign. The District Magistrate had an Ambassador car assigned to him. The Prime Minister also had an Ambassador, but it was fitted with an Isuzu engine. He was driving his own car which was a matter of some concern to us. He stopped at many places in the night and accepted people's applications. His meetings were held at 2 or 3 a.m and there were no crowds at the meetings. The attendance was about equal to the number of police personnel and party workers. We were deeply concerned about security matters all through his visit. When he finally left the borders of Hajipur, all of us heaved a sigh of relief.

There was a plan to link Hajipur to Patna with a bridge over the Ganga. It was very important to link the north, and specially the northwestern districts, of Bihar with Patna. There was only a single bridge linking these two at Mokama. The bridge helped bring people and goods across the Ganga and made things much easier for all concerned. So the traffic on the road connecting Gandhi Bridge increased significantly. There were constant traffic jams in Hajipur and many accidents happened. The basic reason for these accidents was that this road cut through a well-populated district. The people of the village often lived across the road from their land. The village was on one side and the primary school and the primary health care centre on the other. The livestock also had to be taken across the road to their grazing grounds. The cars sped by heedless of all this and after each accident, there would be a traffic jam. The Zilla Parishad had its hands full handling these jams. The main problem was that there was no sidewalk on either side of the road, nor was there an underpass to cross it.

After the bridge was built, several benefits accrued. Many of the officials in Hajipur would commute from Patna. A number of them would leave office at 4 p.m. I had to set up an inspection post on the Gandhi Bridge to prevent these early departures. Many of the operations and functions of the zilla happened before or after working hours. The fact that these officers were not present often created problems. I increased and improved the residential quarters for the officers, the workers and other officials. At that time, the Reserve Officer of Hajipur also frequently came and went from Patna. Once, when he was returning from Patna to Hajipur, there was a huge traffic jam. Saving the inspection of a truck, some policeman had beaten up a driver badly, injuring his face and eyes. In response, the other truck drivers had parked a truck across the road and created a jam. The Reserve Officer's car was stuck in the jam and people began to gherao it.

Although there was a sufficient force at his command, he simply got out of the car and hoofed it to the Circuit House from where he informed me about the jam. At a distance of about three to four kilometres from the Gandhi Bridge, there were three police stations with an adequate number of men. But he thought it best to seek the security of the Circle House and abandon the jam. It was 26 January, Republic Day and there was a cultural programme in which I was participating. That was when I was told of the situation. By the time I got there, the drivers had worked themselves up into a rage. I immediately contacted the Reserve Superintendent and had the two policemen identified and suspended. Thanks to the jam, hundreds of buses and trucks were backed up and the people sitting in them were getting angry. About fifty policemen were present—an adequate force. After instituting an inquiry against the policemen, I sent the injured driver to the hospital in my own car. While I was doing this, my security guard climbed into the truck and moved it out of the way. As soon as this happened, the traffic began to flow again and within thirty minutes, the entire jam had been cleared.

Meanwhile the Reserve Officer's car was overturned and set on fire; the driver had managed to get away. It was late in the night by the time I had all this sorted out. Then I dropped the Reserve Officer to this quarters and went home. It was 1 a.m. by the time I had dinner and went to sleep. At 6 a.m. the phone rang. This was in the days before mobile phones. Half-asleep, I picked up the phone and found that it was the Chief Minister Satyendra Narayan Singh. He asked, 'What's going on? Why has the RO's car been burnt? This is a direct insult to the State.' I replied without thinking that the RO was corrupt and inefficient. There had been no shortage of Reserve Police; he should not have run away from the scene of the incident.

I was sure that there would be an inquiry into his behaviour. But nothing of the sort happened. When the CM came to Vaishali on tour, I was in his car and escorting him to the district border. He said that as we had come this far and we might as well go to the quarters. The RO was already there when we arrived. There were other politicians with him too. They were drinking tea and eating sweetmeats. I realized that the CM was too kind-hearted to institute an inquiry.

I spent a long period of my service—more than three years—at Dhumka. I was the Deputy Commissioner/District Officer there. It was a great opportunity to learn many things and fresh initiatives. When I was running the Literacy Drive in Dhumka, I saw that the Adivasis had a beautiful equation with nature. They were simple but their native intelligence and archives of local knowledge were immense. I remember a time when a group of journalists had come from Delhi and had gone from Dhumka to Sudurvarti village. In one of the villages, the journalists asked an old man to write his name. They wanted to find out whether the Literacy Drive was working, whether the common man could write or not. The man kept on refusing to write his name. They gave him a book and a pen and he returned it. When they insisted again and again, he picked up a stone and wrote his name in the mud. Then he erased it quickly. He said that whenever anyone from the outside had asked him to sign his name or put his thumb impression on a piece paper, he ended up losing some land or a part of his inheritance. The Delhi journalists' faces were a study when they heard this!

It was both easy and difficult to work in the Adivasi areas. It had been their experience that non-Adivasis had taken jobs meant for them or stolen their land and exploited them. When I travelled through the villages for the Literacy Campaign, it took a long time to get people to trust me. It was only after I had eaten and drunk with them, shared in their joys and sorrows and celebrated their festivals with them that they began to trust me. But once they felt sure that I had their best interests at heart, their faith was total. For the three years that I was there, they did not allow any misunderstandings to arise.

Dhumka was certainly a poor, backward and illiterate district but it was replete with natural beauty and the people were simple and hardworking. The Literacy Campaign was an attempt to put an end to the exploitation they faced by making them aware of their rights. Economic aid came from the Central government. The government wanted to expand the remit of the Literacy Campaign at the fundamental level. I believed that literacy could not be its only goal. Districts like Dhumka would not really benefit until literacy was linked to consciousness raising and progress. In many districts where people had learned to read and write a little and where they had become functionally literate and numerate, it had not made much of a change in their lives. Eventually many would relapse into illiteracy. It was our contention that the Literacy Campaign would make sense only if it was linked to making people aware of their rights, made them participants in their own development and progress and improved their economic condition. We also decided that we would not use the traditional methods but adopt their languages, songs and games as tools of education.

Dhumka had a budget of 4 crores for a three-year literacy programme. Because literacy had been linked to progress and consciousness raising, the poor and women participated to a great degree. I wanted to put women front and centre in the programme. I believed that if one woman were to be educated, her entire family would be educated. It was also my experience that if the women understood the programme and saw how it would benefit them their families and society in general, they would become supporters and champions of the programme. In some areas, a few husbands tried to stop their wives from participating. When I went to the villages, I would talk to the men and the women together. I would explain to the men that if their wives and mothers became literate, they would not get 'out of hand'. Their children would be looked after better and they would be able to avail the benefit of government schemes in a more efficient manner.

The literacy campaign run in Dumka was known as the Akil Batti Campaign. It involved nearly a thousand self-help workers, many of whom were women, because we knew this would help to take the campaign to the maximum number of homes. In general, such campaigns in other parts of the country were given very grandiose literary names, using vocabulary that was alien to a vast majority of the people. We had decided that the name and the symbol of our campaign should be kept simple so that no one faced any difficulty in understanding them. We called a meeting of all the stakeholders and asked for suggestions. Seven or eight names were suggested and there were about 300 people to cast their votes. Akil Batti won with the most votes. Dumka had a large Adivasi population. The Santhals were the majority of them. The term 'Akil Batti' is from the Santhali language and it means 'the light of knowledge'. Thus, it became a popular name.

Literacy campaigns were being started in many districts of Bihar and other States as well. This was a campaign initiated by the Central government focusing on adults who were illiterate. Books that they might learn to read were printed at the Centre for distribution to the districts. But when we took a closer look at these books, we did not like them. The names in these books did not sound like the names you would hear in our area. The festivals and fairs described were not very important in Dumka. There were many others which were much more significant for the people there. The pictures seemed alien, as did the people depicted. The first line of the first book read: *'Bharatvarsha ke sheersh par Himalaya ka taj hai'* (The Himalayas are the crown on India's head). The target audience in Dumka might have heard of 'Bharatvarsha' but most had no idea what the Himalayas were and what a crown was—their geography and their ideas of society and rulers were very different.

The books also talked about festivals like Holi, Deepavali and Durga Puja while the Adivasis celebrated other festivals. The characters in the stories did not have familiar names and the pictures used in them were not from their areas. The language of the books was too literary and alien and therefore, difficult to understand. So we decided to change the books we would use in the Literacy Campaign. We decided that we would create our own books which would be written by local writers. The language would be simple and the illustrations, names and incidents would be local and relatable. We chose to write about local fairs and festivals, great personalities of the region, local crops and even diseases. These books became very popular and helped us a great deal in our work.

The scheme was an unprecedented success as people began to see the change it could make in their lives. They understood the concept of minimum wages and refused to accept less. Meetings were held about various government schemes and they began to choose the schemes they felt were needed. Committees were set up to keep tabs on implementation and the members were trained in keeping accounts, log books and journals. Some of the schemes were simplified. Earlier, when houses were built for the poor, they were constructed far away from their homes by contractors. Most of these were never used since the beneficiaries did not leave their old homes, their cattle and the area they were familiar with. Now the people were told to build their houses up by two hundred feet and to take the money from us. This house-building scheme was conducted in the names of the women. The right to measure was also given—besides to the engineer—to the workers and panchayat officials as well.

In order to increase the involvement of the women, one job was assigned to the woman's committee in every panchayat. The department raised the issue that they lacked experience in buying bricks, cement, sand and other building materials. We replied that people buy all this material when they build their own homes so why could they not purchase these things for small construction projects like schools, aanganwadis and bus stops?

In order to popularize the saving habit, Dadi Banks were opened in every village, in which the village women could deposit their savings or take loans from when they needed them. The only things each bank got from the government were a metal box and a register. The women of the village often needed money for small incidental expenses such as medicines, clothes or books for children. If they wanted to start a small business, they had to have starting capital. Earlier, they had to go to the village money lender for these. Now they could get the money in the village itself. Dadi Banks were not commercial establishments. Money was available at any time of the day and night and even on public holidays. These banks proved so popular that eventually a huge amount of money was accumulated and in them and the supervision had to be increased. Commercial banks began to say that such banks should not be allowed but we persisted because they served the people's needs.

Small businesses like kitchen gardening, poultry farming and goat herding were popularized among the women. This created a new awareness in them and a desire to be entrepreneurs. They began to compete with each other to start these businesses. If there was injustice, oppression or corruption, they were fought with vigour.

One of the major problems of Dhumka was drinking water. The government had set up many hand pumps in the villages but most of them had stopped working because they needed minor repairs. Women were trained in repairing the pumps and they were given mechanical tools and cycles. These women would charge a small amount to repair the hand pumps. They became so famous that a film was made about them which was shown at the Lal Bahadur Shastri IAS Training Academy.

One year, we got funds for planting 5 lakh fruit-bearing trees. A scheme for their distribution was made. It was decided that if a girl had been born in any family, they would be entitled to anywhere between five or ten fruit bearing saplings, depending on the availability of land.

The women had a mobility problem. Often it was difficult for them to go to the panchayat, the block office or for training sessions. We started a scheme with 5 lakhs as seed money by which women could borrow the money to buy a cycle and repay the sum in a year and many women, among whose number there were some Dalits, began to learn how to cycle. This cycle scheme became very popular. Many people would load sacks of coal from the godowns on to their cycles and sell the coal in the local markets. I would often see them dragging their cycles up hill and down dale, all over Dhumka. They would carry these sacks and make one or more trips to the market.

I once had a meeting with these people and they told me how difficult their work became during the rains and in the summer since there was no place for them to stop for a breather and have a drink of water. Then the officials of the Central Coalfield Ltd or the police would harass them. I told the Central Coalfield Ltd officials that they needed to streamline the processes of coal mining and provide these youths with coal at the minimum possible prices so that they might earn their living. But I knew this would not happen. I created rest areas for them in four different places with hand pumps to provide drinking water. Seeing my concern for them, the police also backed off and left them alone.

At the Mahila Mahotsav which I organized in Dhumka, more than 500 sportspeople and sports officials took part. In a small town, we had to put up so many people and provide good sports grounds and practice spaces. This was the first time such a big programme was happening in Dhumka. I called people from the city and appealed for help. The city took up the challenge to run a campaign to clean it up. Houses were painted or whitewashed. They also took on the responsibility of providing refreshments at the various centres.

There were many kinds of industries around Dhumka who were invited to participate in the event. When a big industrialist sent a donation of twenty-five thousand rupees, I felt a little uncomfortable. I asked the staff of the district (leaving out the Class IV staff) if they would help. I had expected a contribution of about two hundred rupees from each individual. Within a few days, they contributed 22 lakhs. Then a representative of the Class IV staff came to meet me to ask why they had not been invited to contribute. I said that this was because their salaries were lower than that of the others and I had not wanted to subject them to any economic deprivation. He told me that they saw this as a matter of honour for their district and for them. They came up with a contribution of a hundred rupees each. I returned the rather small amounts that the industrialists had given explaining that the workers themselves had brought in enough money to conduct the programme. It also taught me a lesson in people power.

We had asked the newly literate women to open accounts in the nearby post office under the Mahila Samriddhi Yojana (Micro Finance Scheme for Women). Under this scheme, if a woman deposited seventy-five rupees the government would contribute twenty-five. I wanted these women to get used to filling forms and to learn the importance of their signatures. I also wanted them to go to a government office and get a passbook. However, the number of women was too high for the post offices of the area to handle. And so, the post offices were asked to open a booth at the local haat where the women could open their accounts. As a result, Dhumka was judged the best performer in the Mahila Samriddhi Yojana and we received a cheque of 5 lakhs as well.

During the Akil Batti Campaign, an organization called Jaago Behna (Sisters, Awake!) was established in every block of the district. The women were made aware of the problems that might arise from remaining illiterate. They were paid less for their labour. Being unaware of government schemes that were meant for them, they could not avail of the benefits and they often had to take the help of middlemen. They could not raise their voices to express their needs or the needs of their society. They could not fight the alcoholism rampant among the men. Not could they ensure the health of their children or their access to a good education. Although both education and medical attention had been made free, there was a shortage of doctors and nurses in the hospitals and of teachers and books in the schools. They found it difficult to band together and to access markets for their goods. Because they had low incomes, they had almost no savings. And so, any unexpected incidental expenses forced them to turn to the village moneylender who charged exorbitant rates of interest.

These women were put in charge of monitoring the Literacy Campaign. They undertook a mission to fight social evils such as child marriage and dowry. Two hundred to three hundred women leaders were born out of this campaign in the entire district. They began to take an active role in local politics. Regular elections were also held for the posts of officials in the Jaago Behna campaign so that the right women might enter the campaign.

Once, there was an election in Ranishwar block. There were two women from the same family who were very enthusiastic and committed. I wanted only one of the two to be elected to the committee so that others might also get a chance. To make sure of this, I had some IAS trainees sent down there with an escort of three or four policemen. Seeing them, the women who had gathered for the election got angry and told the trainees and the policemen to go back. They said that it was their election and they would not allow interference of any kind. And both the women of that family in Ranishwar won the election.

A similar incident happened when I was setting up the local women workers committee. Two women had to be chosen for the committee. A hundred women gathered at the office, asking to be chosen. It was going to be a difficult pick. I had an office on the second floor of the Literacy Campaign building. I announced that any woman who agreed to jump from the second floor would be chosen. Nine women agreed. They were chosen as candidates and the others elected two of them after casting their votes.

The media played an important role in the Literacy Campaign. Those in the media were local residents and so it was their responsibility to participate in it. They would of course monitor its progress from the outside and administer correctives where necessary, but I thought it would make greater sense if they got involved in it. When the committee was being set up, we had local media representatives as members of the environmental committee, the documentation committee and even the finance committee. This way, they could see for themselves whether the right slates had come in or whether the notebooks were of good quality. This was the first time that the media had been embedded in a government campaign and so they worked with responsibility and enthusiasm.

Then it occurred to me that all the press notices and

cuttings about the Literacy Campaign should be collected. I thought that collating them in a book might be a good idea. This would not only provide evidence of external evaluation of the programme but would also serve as a reminder of what happened when. The cuttings were organized and published in a book titled *Surkhiyon Mein Saaksharta* (Literacy in the Headlines). Only published pieces were included in exactly the same way as they had been printed. There were many articles that were critical of the programme but we featured those as well. This provided a chronological record of the starting of the programme, its development and its successes. We also discovered that some of those who had joined in the hope of finding fame or quick profits soon moved away. Others who had not joined in the beginning did so later and worked with enthusiasm and brought their expertise to the programme. The book became very popular and was much in demand in other districts where the Literacy Campaign was running.

The workers of the Literacy Campaign also decided to bring out a newspaper of their own. Each district would produce its own edition. The news would be gathered and written by the women and those who were able to would edit the material. I asked the editor of the Patna edition of *Dainik Hindustan* to bring his team to Dhumka to train our aspiring journalists.

They conducted a two-way workshop with the trainees. The editor, Sunil Dubey, was so impressed by the women that he said his team had learned a lot from the women too.

Some rules were set for these local newspapers. There would be no praise printed of any minister or local official who might be a supervisory officer of any of the Literacy Campaign workers. This newspaper was for the Literacy Campaign workers to write about the experiments conducted in their districts or about the progress that had been made thanks to the campaign. In the beginning, it was decided to print a thousand copies of each newspaper in every district. The district would give a rupee per copy in economic support. It was anticipated that within three months, people would begin to buy their own papers and the papers would become self-supporting. The newspapers became very popular and people began to read photostat copies as well. They carried only news about the Literacy Campaign and its workers. To see their names in the papers was a revelation and a source of encouragement to them. Some of the papers even carried critical reports of the processes of the district office. One of them berated me saying that I should pay more attention to the Literacy Campaign.

Sunil Dubey was so impressed by the newspapers of Dhumka that he expressed the desire to carry Dhumka news in the editorial of *Hindustan*. We managed to send him about fifteen to twenty pieces, all of which were featured prominently. Later he told me that the circulation of *Hindustan* had increased substantially in Dhumka thanks to those reports.

One day, several women of the Jaago Behna came to meet me in my residential office at 10.30 a.m. I had returned late the previous night from a district tour and so I slept late that morning. I was having a bath when the women arrived. They waited for a while but then they said that I did not get paid to bathe at 10.30 in the morning. I ought to be in the office on time. I was delighted at this evidence of an awakening to their rights as citizens.

The Jamtara block in Dhumka had a teacher called K. Sushila who had taken up a leadership role in the campaign. A huge Literacy Campaign rally was organized in Jamtara. A day earlier, she had suffered a miscarriage. When we went to offer our condolences, we found the committed leader at work with the others, preparing for the rally.

The Jaago Behna women would go into the villages of the district located in mountainous areas where the Literacy Campaign had not gathered momentum. They would spend ten to fifteen days there and make sure things were functioning properly before they returned. One of the women was bitten by a snake and died. She was a Christian and we buried her with full State honours. I was present along with the Reserve Officer and other senior functionaries.

In another incident, boys from a rich family had raped an adolescent girl from the dhobi community. After raping her, they dumped her body in a dry well thinking she was dead. The people of the neighbouring area heard the cries of the half-dead girl. She was rescued and taken to a hospital.

The Jaago Behna women called for an emergency meeting. I was on my way to the office when I heard about the meeting. The Saksharta Bhavan was somewhere between my office and my residence. I went there to attend the meeting. Some of the women stepped out of the meeting and said that I should not attend. It was opposing the district administration and they would come with their demands to the administrative offices later. I reminded them that I was chairman of the Jaago Behna organization. To which one of the women replied that it was sometimes necessary to oppose the chairman too.

The women of Jaago Behna closed down the entire market and blocked the entry and exit roads. They gave us twenty-four hours to arrest the rapists. Then the women took out a mammoth procession, in which, to everyone's surprise, the womenfolk of the family of the accused men took part. The police formed three teams and gave orders to carry out an immediate arrest. Late in the night, the man was arrested in a hotel room in the nearby city of Devghar. They wanted to present him in court at 10 a.m. the next day. They kept him in the lock-up at Dhumka for the night. The news spread like wildfire and hundreds of women turned up to give him a sound beating with their chappals and shoes. At that time, there was no fear of violating human rights nor were there as many televisions channels as there are today.

In any case, this murderous criminal was sentenced to a jail term. The women kept up the pressure on the courts so that not a single lawyer in Dhumka would move a bad plea. The Jaago Behna women sent the survivor to a missionary hospital so that she might receive proper medical attention. We wanted to contribute to her care but the women refused. They would collect the money themselves.

A simple book was prepared about the solutions to such problems as well as the programmes that might benefit women. The processes by which one might bring schemes of social development to one's village were described. People were trained to monitor the execution of social development programmes. The minimum wage in every employment scheme was published so that if anyone tried to pay less, they might be able to oppose this exploitation and expose such corruption. Small groups were started with a business or a project each and given some working capital.

Dhumka was declared Bihar's first literate district. Bihar did not use people's groups to run the Literacy Campaign as was the case in Kerala and other southern states. Here the government went directly to the people to run it. We knew that it would take a while to organize a good people's movement. We could not wait for that to happen and it was my contention that we needed self-motivated workers more than self-help groups. Another important factor was that the people of Dhumka were running the Literacy Campaign for their brothers, sisters, fathers, uncles and mothers. The government workers and the teachers were also from Dhumka and a desire to bring about social change and awareness was instilled in them.

From the money we received for the Literacy Campaign, we got about 20 lakhs as interest. I used this amount to set up a Literacy Bhavan in Dhumka. The Government of India in collaboration with UNICEF announced the Satyen Mitra National Award for work done in literacy campaigns across the nation. The district of Dhumka won the first Satyen Maitra Award. On the one hand, we won this award and on the other, we had an audit conducted by the Accountant General which said that at the end of the Literacy Campaign, Dhumka had not become a hundred per cent literate while all the funds allocated had been spent. At the end of the campaign, the percentage of the literate had gone from 30 to 60 per cent. In my reply, I asked how it was possible for Dhumka to win an award as the best Literacy Campaign in the country and still attract unfavourable comment from the Accountant General. The report also found the Bhavan to be improper in its work process. It was their opinion that the interest should have been returned to the government. Anyway, this discussion went on for quite a while but perhaps it has now been laid to rest.

The people however, found the campaign interesting and were inspired by it. They began to feel that I might be of some use to them and if I were to stay there, we might even see some progress. So they made inquiries about my salary and how much longer I would be in service. At that time and at those rates, I could expect to earn 1 crore and 70 lakhs if I stuck to my job. Dhumka had 17 lakh residents. They made me an offer. They would gather ten rupees from each resident of Dhumka and give me 1 crore and 70 lakhs so that I might quit my job and take over the Literacy Campaign leadership. It was also suggested that they would build me an ashram on the Kurua mountain.

This was a real surprise. I had discovered that a campaign like this could have remarkable side effects, bringing about consciousness among the people and giving them the incentive to take up causes and to fight injustice. But it is precisely then that it is challenging to provide leadership. Governmental organizations find it difficult to contain this energy and disappointment sets in. People change and so do their mindsets but the government lacks the flexibility to respond effectively. After three years at Dhumka, I was transferred. Even though I had been offered my entire salary of a lifetime and accommodation, I could not stay.

I went as Commissioner to the Purnia division and was posted as the Commissioner of the Tirhat division too. I had some experience of Purnia, having worked there as a probationer in 1982–83. Not much had changed although the Purnia division was new. One of the major responsibilities of the Divisional Commissioner was the legal aspect since he constituted the court of appeal to which petitioners could come if they did not accept the decisions of the district officers. But I found that there were very few appeals and so I gave up the idea of a daily court sitting and fixed two days for the appeals. When I asked my clerk why the appeals were so few, he replied that it would only be when the District Officers actually heard matters and gave decisions that people could appeal. When I investigated this, I found that the majority of the officers were not holding court. I fixed a day for the hearing of matters and asked for a monthly report as well.

In the past, the post of District Commissioner was a prize given to the preferred candidates of the IAS. He exercised control over a large area. This was why distant areas had Camp Courts so that people did not have to travel too far in search of justice. Gradually, the number of districts and divisions increased and some divisions took on two districts as well. With improvements in travel facilities, Camp Courts came to an end and the officers held them in their head offices.

The roads in Purnia were notorious. At one point of time, I was given additional charge of Koshi Division, Saharsa. My clerk organized two cars when I was setting out. When I asked him why, he said that the road between

Purnia and Saharsa was very bad. Unheeding, I set off in a single car and, of course, twenty to twenty-five kilometres into our journey, the car's axle broke. The roads were deeply scarred with potholes for miles in both directions. Since they had not been repaired for a long time, the potholes were now craters. My clerk organized another car from the next block to pick me up and I finally reached Saharsa. When I was returning, we found two trucks parked on the road. On inquiring, we were told that they had been halted by some goons who had stolen their money and made away with it. I ordered my driver to chase the goons but they were on motorbikes and we could not catch them.

Later, I asked around how people got from Saharsa to Purnia and was told about a local train that ran between the two. The locals also informed me that when officers were given additional charge, they too used the train.

Fish was available in plenty in Purnia since two rivers ran through it: the Ganga and the Koshi. Many Himalayan streams flowed through it too. Purnia also had many lakes and ponds in which mud-eating fish such as the singhi, the mangoor and the kevaii lived in large numbers.

When I first went to Purnia, I was told the story of a Bengali Commissioner who loved eating fish. A down-to-earth gentleman, he would go to the market to buy his fish. His was a small family so he bought only a few. When they saw him coming, the fishmongers took fright for he would ask for five hundred grams of some large fish. Bihari fishmongers think a kilo is an acceptable amount of fish and here was a gentleman who would ask for anything between two-hundred to five-hundred grams. And when you want a good cut from a big fish, it is expected that you should ask for at least two kilos.

I had a friend in Purnia called Khokhan Dada who worked in the Life Insurance Corporation of India. He too was a great one for fish. His job was to go to the market each morning and to buy fish for himself and for me. One day, he told me that it was getting difficult to get good fish in the Purnia markets since dealers from Siliguri would swoop down before 8 a.m. and buy up all the good fish. So I made a decision that dealers from Siliguri could only buy fish at Purnia after 8 a.m. Purnia residents ought by rights to have the first pick of Purnia's fish markets.

Being the Divisional Commissioner of Tirhut (Muzzafarpur) was a slightly different experience. If Purnia was a sleepy district, Muzaffarpur was alive and vibrant. As a city Muzaffarpur was much livelier.

The quarters of the Commissioner in Muzaffarpur were called Laal Kothi (the Red House). After the Governor's House at Patna, it was the largest residential quarters. It had a huge ball room and many reception halls. Upstairs, there were dozens of rooms. Beneath the dancing floor was a water body, installed by the British, to keep the ballroom cool. Keeping this huge building clean and maintaining it was a problem. We closed most of the rooms and opened only a few that we lived in. I told my superiors that this white elephant should be put to better use: as a college or some other institution. A smaller and more manageable residence could easily be built somewhere in the same area.

In comparison to Purnia, Muzaffarpur had many matters that needed attention and the courts had much work to do.

Most of this concerned land and there was no shortage of lawyers. I increased the number of sports, art and cultural activities. I also introduced the Tirhut Festival. We held an international Kabaddi competition as well.

During my time there, the Boodi Gandak flooded, affecting the lives of thousands of people. When I was organizing the distribution of relief material, it came to my attention that an MLA wanted to take two-thirds of all the material that had been sent by the State government when his ward was only entitled to one-tenth of it. I said that this was wrong and I would not allow it. He and his constituency would get its fair share and no more. This enraged the honourable MLA and he went to Patna and got me transferred. Later, I even thanked him for this. Suspecting me of irony, he tried to explain away his actions.

5

Five Years at the Centre

I went to New Delhi on deputation in 1998. Perhaps it was my bio-data that made them place me in the Human Resource Development department at Mantralaya. In the State, I had been promoted to Secretary level. My batchmates at the Centre were at the level of Director. And so, my deputation was also at the same level.

However, before I could go to Delhi, I had to secure my release from the Bihar cadre and this was not without its attendant difficulties. When I received the deputation order, I applied to the Personnel and Administrative Reforms department for the transfer (it had another name then). When I heard nothing for fifteen days, I went to meet Devashish Gupta, the Secretary of the department. I told him that the deputation order stated that if I did not present myself in fifteen days, the order would be rendered null and void.

He said, 'Sit down, have a cup of tea. Consider yourself lucky if you can get away in a month.' He explained that I would have to meet the Chief Minister and get his permission to go to Delhi. This was the tradition in Bihar. He also told me what the Chief Minister was going to say and what I must say in response. The Chief Minister would say that if all the good IAS officers went to Delhi, who would be left in Bihar? My response was to be that I wanted to go there for my children's education. And I should add that every IAS officer has to spend some time at the Centre or face difficulties in the matter of future promotions and appointments.

At that time, I had a friend called Abdul Bari Siddiqui. I asked him to organize a meeting with the Chief Minister. Siddiqui Sahab obliged and I met the then Chief Minister, Laloo Prasad Yadav. Our conversation ran exactly along the lines predicted by Mr Gupta. I got my relieving order the next day.

I joined the Ministry of Education as Director. I was given the task of heading the Directorate of Vocational Education perhaps because I had considerable experience with the Literacy Campaign in Bihar. I was also given the task of supervising training and monitoring. In those days, I was in the habit of chewing paan. The first problem I encountered was that there were no spittoons anywhere. The second was that there was no car to take me to office and back. Nor was there anyone to bring you a cup of tea or a glass of water if you wanted one. You had to go to the cafeteria for the former and to the water-cooler for the latter. We had grown used to this service in Bihar. And although it bothered me at first, I got used to the new dispensation quite soon. I had a Deputy Secretary, two Branch Officers and other assorted assistants working under me.

On the first day, I received a file that was written in beautiful English with many perceptive comments. I was rather overawed by this; how could my subordinates have such a clear grasp of these concepts and how was it possible that they were expressing themselves with such conciseness and perspicacity? Within the next fortnight however, I found out the secret. There were computers everywhere and the Internet was in great demand. Whatever the subject, the officers had recourse to the Internet and would simply cut and paste the comments they were supposed to make. I was forced to disconnect the computers we were using from the Internet.

Some of the Joint Secretaries would work until late at night. They seemed to start work at around 5 p.m. At around 5.30, their colleagues would leave for home. Someone explained that these gentlemen did not want to go home until it was late and so they found excuses to work late. I was not used to idling my time away so I began to think of new things I could do in this new area. The government's decision-making process was very complex. In the beginning, I would grow impatient at the delays, but slowly I got used to this as well.

My friends said that if I managed a couple of new things during my five-year stint at the Centre, I should think of it as time well spent.

While I was looking after those with special needs at the Ministry of Social Justice, I started a new scheme. It was to set up a centre for people with special needs in every district. When we conducted a survey of various States, we found that people with special needs had been marginalized. Their problems could not be resolved in any one place and so they had to go from one place to another. What we wanted was to provide a centre in every district which could cater to all their needs. Those with special needs would receive a certificate stating that they were so challenged. They should have facilities for rehabilitation and there should be an attempt to provide them with some way of earning a living as this would give them a certain amount of respect in society. The minister approved the scheme. We did not ask for a huge sum and so within a year, the scheme could be implemented across the country.

The other important problem that presented itself was the position of those afflicted by mental illness. At that time, the Central government had passed the Persons with Disabilities Act 2005. Several disabilities, including being visually challenged, hearing impaired or mobility challenged had been covered by the Act. The Central government estimated that 3 per cent of the nation's population faced a variety of challenges and thus found it difficult to step into the national mainstream. There were arrangements for their education, health and employment. Earlier, there would be many who were physically challenged due to polio. Others were visually challenged—either blind or having reduced vision. Adults and children alike suffered hearing loss. There were those who could not speak. Many schemes and organizations such as Alimco had been set up already. As the nation progressed, some of these infirmities and disabilities such as the incidence of mobility loss due to polio began to decrease.

The government had set up organizations to help people

with disabilities and it also encouraged the setting up of self-help organizations. In this regard, I toured most parts of the country to study the situation. I found that physical disabilities had reduced but the number of adults and children suffering from mental disabilities had increased. Yet, the Act did not cover mental disabilities or challenges. Perhaps the rationale was that the government did not have the resources to cover both and so physical disability was given priority. Besides, there was not much awareness about mental health issues and it was commonly considered a condition that affected the wealthy. But a tour of the country made it clear that paying attention to mental health issues could not be postponed.

There were some self-help organizations in Maharashtra, Karnataka and Kerala that were working on these issues. I visited these organizations. The Centre also went through a series of high-level discussions and the National Trust Act was passed. This was to make provisions for education, health and employment for the mentally challenged, especially children, for whom early intervention was vital if they were to become self-sufficient and productive members of society. Some mentally challenged children had no guardians and they had to be provided for too. The National Trust Act appointed a Secretary in the Central government who would be in charge of these efforts. One of the most important changes was the introduction of training for medical staff—including everyone from doctors to paramedics—specifically in the area of mental disability, and schemes to help the mentally challenged enter the national mainstream.

At that time, Maneka Gandhi was the Minister. All the department officials lived in fear of her because she was known to be a hard taskmaster and wanted everything done very fast. When the work did not happen at the speed she expected, her language was unrestrained. When the Honourable Minister asked an official how much time was needed for a task, the bureaucrat would reply in terror that it would take fifteen days even if, in reality, a month was needed. The Minister would reply that a fortnight was far too long and demand that it be completed in a week. And if she did not receive the report in a week, her emails and telephone calls would begin. When she asked me how much time something would take. I would say that we would need to give the matter considerable thought and also do a lot of research and so it would take a month. The Honourable Minister would then give me fifteen days as was her habit. And generally, that would be sufficient time.

The other technique was not to fear. Generally, review meetings meant that the officials sat quietly with their heads bowed while the Honourable Minister spoke and spoke. I found that I had no problem in meeting her gaze when I talked to her. I realized that the Minister found routine work boring and wanted to do new things. I too wanted to do new things and so I would present her with novel ideas and schemes.

The role of the personal secretary is one of great importance in the Central government. My first personal secretary was a Punjabi woman who was fashionable and very health-conscious. All day long, she ate fruits and salads and drank juices. I would bring my tiffin from home which was generally roti, bhujiya and salad. She found my meals rather surprising. Once she even told my wife that I should have more protein and less carbohydrates. Anyway, she was soon transferred.

My second personal secretary was a very methodical person. He was from Kerala and had worked in a minister's office before. His work was extremely systematic. He had an important position in the cadre of personal secretaries. There were three or four reasons why my friends in Delhi and those who came to Patna might seek me out. Since I was in the Human Resource Development Ministry, they would come to me for help with their children's admission. Another group approached me on health grounds, having come from Patna to Delhi to seek medical help. Some wanted assistance with railway ticket confirmations and some friends came on sightseeing tours and shopping trips. My personal secretary had created standard drafts for those seeking admission or medical assistance. He would fill in the blanks and present them to me for my signature. When I would ask him what happened about the admission, he could say that our job was to provide the letter and it was the applicant's responsibility to make the best of use of it. I found this rather strange because in Bihar, one did not rest until the job was done.

My personal secretary had the foresight to maintain a list of the names and phone numbers of all those who had been given recommendations by me. So if I had given a railway officer a recommendation letter for his child's admission, he would call the officer up when we had a railway ticket to confirm.

Once, I wanted to meet a very senior official. I asked my personal secretary if he could arrange an appointment in the next ten to fifteen days. The next day, he called to say I could meet him and then go to my office. This came as a surprise. Later, he told me that the personal secretaries had a network and he had put in a word and secured an appointment for me.

Many of the Central government officers got the opportunity to do their MBAs abroad under the Commonwealth scholarships. I put in an application too. Selection was based on one's seniority and character. When the list came out, I found my name on the waiting list. I did not know that the selection of candidates was not in the hands of the Australian government; it had been outsourced to a private organization called Aus Aid. I knew the head official at Aus Aid well. Many of the programmes at the Human Resource Development Ministry were conducted with Aus Aid assistance. When he heard that I was on the waiting list, he told me that I was not to worry, I was on my way Down Under. Since we had worked closely together, he was a good friend. He began to ask the Personnel Ministry a series of questions: why were there so few women on the list? Where was the representation of the underprivileged? The Ministry found it difficult to answer these. He made it clear to the Ministry that as long as my name was not on the list, it would not be accepted.

And so it came to pass that my name appeared on the list and I set off for Australia to do my MBA. Since he knew of my love of nature, my friend chose a university in New South Wales which was surrounded by jungles.

As a Director in the Central government, I found that I was doing the work of a well-paid clerk. Though I wanted to do many things, I could not. The condition in the States was different. There, if you wanted to work, you could achieve a lot and you could do it quickly too. It was possible to benefit the people quickly while this was not the case at the centre. The one good thing that came out of my time at the Centre was that I got to travel the length and breadth of the country.

For a while, I was even in charge of yoga. In this position, I made a survey of almost all the important yoga centres, met a wide range of people and made many friends. I saw a range of different State programmes. At the time, there was also a great deal of respect for the officials from the Central government. One could meet the State's ministers and secretaries easily. This has slowly begun to change.

The IAS officers at the Centre were often called 'mobile assets' in jest. They come on deputation for a fixed period and then leave. However, there are also those who stay on in their department. They are called 'permanent assets', again, in fun. These permanent assets also have a strong network and secure the best jobs for themselves. The officers from Bihar are seen as good fits for the difficult and tricky assignments.

My quarters in Delhi were in Kaka Nagar, not far from the office at Shastri Bhavan. I wanted a house with some land attached so I could do a bit of gardening. I got a ground floor flat with a good amount of land in front. The summer in Delhi is hot and dry and so we bought our first cooler. Mobiles were available then but they were expensive.

Coming to Delhi, we discovered that your house came with a water meter and you paid a municipal tax for it. The drinking water supply in Kaka Nagar was salty so drinking water had to be brought home from the office each day. We had a car in which my children went to school and I went to the office. My children were young and so we had them admitted to a school near Kaka Nagar. They would wonder why we had only one car while our neighbours had many. At Diwali and the New Year, man gifts would arrive at the neighbours' homes while all gifts were refused at ours. My children could scarcely believe I was an IAS officer for we had none of the comforts of Bihar in Delhi. Their friends' birthdays were celebrated at farm houses or restaurants; theirs were celebrated at home. Through my entire career, it was only when I was posted in Delhi that my salary combined with the income from my wife's job, was not sufficient to make ends meet. At the end of every month, we had to tighten our belts.

Once, a minister came to Delhi from Bihar. He wanted to meet a minister from the Central government who was also from Bihar. I told the minister from Bihar that nothing in Delhi works without a middleman. Everyone is connected to some middleman or the other who manages all their family affairs. He will get their children admitted to school, get their ration cards issued, fix the gas connection and do whatever else needs to be done. The minister from Bihar said that he did not believe everyone did this and so we placed a bet. We were going to the minister's house and I said we would meet someone of this kind, a fixer, there. The Central minister was a man of honour with an untarnished image. The Bihar minister said that the Central minister would not be like that and was willing to lose a hundred rupees.

When we arrived at the minister's office in his quarters, we met a Sardar ji who was making entries of all those who sought to meet the minister. I had been told that in Delhi, even promotion to the higher ranks happens through these middlemen. Initially, I did not believe it. How could the middlemen be so influential? But then at one point in time, a senior officer of the IAS was appointed to the post of Chairman and Managing Director of the Food Corporation of India. I knew him as a Secretary of the HRD Ministry. He was indubitably a man of integrity and hard working too. I asked how he came to be appointed. I was told that there was a lobby pushing for X to be appointed and was spending money to secure the post for him while another lobby was doing the same for Y. When neither lobby found enough traction, a third party was chosen. Both lobbies seemed to be satisfied: X's lobby had the grim satisfaction of knowing that Y had not been chosen and Y's lobby was also satisfied that X had failed.

6

From Sachivalaya to the Chief Minister's Office

I have been variously posted to the Health department, the Finance department, the Cabinet Secretariat, the Bihar Education Project, the Education department and the Agriculture department. When I was in the Education Project, I was given full charge of Art, Culture and Youth. From 2014 to 2018, I was Chief Secretary. After retirement in 2018, I was made Advisor to the Chief Minister.

In the Finance department, I was also Director of the Treasury. Laloo Prasad Yadav was the Chief Minister at that time. In March, a newspaper printed a story about the 'March Loot'. This was a reference to the fact that in the month of March, huge sums of money came through the various departments. What was wont to happen was that in the beginning of the financial year, the expenditure would be slow and towards the end of the year, huge amounts would be spent to exhaust the budgetary allocations. There was a meeting at the Chief Minister's office at which the Solicitor General, the Chief Secretary, the Finance Commissioner and other senior officials were present. It was decided that the expenditures incurred by different departments would be analyzed. At the time, all the accounts of the Directorate of Accounts were hand-written; this was before computers and sophisticated software were available. The Finance department wanted to tell the Chief Minister that it would take some time to gather and present all the expenditures made by the various departments. However, it was my contention that if the government wanted, it could make this happen.

The accounts from various districts began to flow into my directorate in huge sacks. To make the accounting easier, a list of expenses was created and all bills in excess of 1 crore were separated. The main auditorium of the Secretariat was turned into a space where the analysis was to be done and the Chief Secretaries and Finance Secretaries and officers of the various departments were also present. It emerged that Chaibasa district's Animal Husbandry department had spent an unusually large sum of money in March. The district official made some reply when questioned, but it was not a satisfactory answer. And so, it was decided that the district officials should make a detailed account of all expenditure and on the basis of that, an investigation would be launched. A little after this I was made the Deputy District Collector of Dhumka. I called a meeting of all the different departments of the district at which the Treasury officers were present and made it clear that I would tolerate no irregular expenditure on my watch. If anyone tried to fudge accounts, stern action would be taken. As a result, as long as I was the Deputy District Collector, the only expenditures incurred were on the wage bill and other small expenses.

Once, a Treasury official sent me a file about a small expenditure. He wanted me to sign off on it, which was quite surprising. He was entitled to sanction such an amount. I wrote on the file that in the future, he should only forward sums of over a lakh of rupees for approval; he could clear anything less at his level. Frankly speaking, I did not have the right to create such a rule but I had only issued the order to prevent the misuse of large sums of money. Later, the State Animal Husbandry official overrode this but I was not told about it. And the Dhumka Treasury officials began to pass large sums of money.

Some months later, an order arrived from the Finance department. It had come to their notice that the Animal Husbandry department's expenditures exceeded the budgetary allocations made for it. I received an order asking me to investigate. From the investigation it became clear that huge sums of money had been taken out illegally. Sums had been paid for supplies that had never turned up; false truck numbers had been assigned. More money had been taken out than had been allocated. The investigation went on for two days after which I made the decision that this would have to be a criminal case. Then I received a message from the Finance department that a special team would be sent and they would conduct the investigation themselves. It was not possible for me to obey this order. Dhumka was a small town in which a huge scam had been uncovered by the District Collector. Hence, it was important that a criminal case be filed without further delay.

Dhumka became the first district to initiate criminal proceedings in the infamous fodder scam. At first the police investigated it, but soon a decision was taken that the CBI should lead the investigation. It was also decided that the CBI investigation should be supervised by a bench of the Patna High Court. This investigation went on for a long time. The CBI made me a witness in the case. The investigating officers did not have much experience of handling this kind of case and it took them a while to understand the mechanics of it.

What was then eastern Bihar (and is now Jharkhand) had the majority of these unjustified expenditures. It became clear that the District Collectors played no real role in the whole. A summary of the expenditures was presented on a monthly basis to the District Collector who signed it and sent it to the Accountant General. When I was District Collector in Vaishali I would send these summaries to the Accountant General. When such a summary was not presented to me in Vaishali, I asked why. Since I had sent a written query, I received a written reply. The Treasury officer of Dhumka replied, in writing, that the Treasury officers signed the monthly expenditure summaries and sent them to the Accountant General who accepted them. This tradition had been carrying on for years. And so, the monthly summary was not sent in Dhumka at my level. Eventually the CBI sent a request to the State government to conduct departmental inquiries against all those District Collectors in whose districts these unwarranted expenditures had taken place. I too was investigated and the procedure took many long years. When it finally ended, I came to the conclusion that I would have to be more vigilant in the future.

A complex scheme had been devised to conceal the

fodder scam. The Animal Husbandry department had used the available monies to it and had created different disposal officers. Just as the Treasury officers could sanction a payment, these Animal Husbandry department officers could also sanction payments. And so, the extra-judicial payments were all made through these officers. Copies of these payments were not sent to the Audit department. And hence, it was difficult to keep track of these payments. I was completely sure that the Animal Husbandry department of Dhumka was not making any large payments but how could I know that these payments were being made, circumventing the usual channels?

One day, the Commissioner of Santhal Pargana informed me that he wanted to carry out an inspection of the accounts at Dhumka. Later, I discovered that they wanted to intimidate the department with the threat of an inspection into doing other works for them. The Animal Husbandry department was now so powerful that the Audit department officials told me that the Commissioner, Dhumka could not inspect the auditors. According to the rules, only the sub-divisional Treasury had the right to perform such an inspection, not the District Treasury. This made me angry. I said that I was certainly entitled to do it since I was a District Treasury official. Anyway, the investigation did happen and on the basis of this, a confidential report was prepared. This report was taken to Patna but he was told, at some level, that it would not be wise to file this report and it should be withdrawn. Later, the Commissioner had to go to jail for having circumvented my orders; there were other charges against him as well. The fodder scam and the cases related to it dragged on through the courts for the next twenty to twenty-five years and some are still to be heard. The majority have been decided; a few are left.

In 2004, I went as Secretary to the Cabinet Secretariat which is tasked with the implementation of decisions taken at the ministerial level. It also involved organizing tours of Bihar for prominent international and national visitors and the supervision of the Bihar Bhavans and the State Archives.

At that time, there wasn't much by way of decentralization in Bihar. Any scheme of over 25 lakhs had to be approved at the Ministry level. This meant a logjam of proposals awaiting sanction at the Ministries. In 2004, this seemed unacceptably anachronistic to me. Later, the bar was raised so that schemes of above 20 crores only had to have ministerial sanction. All the Departmental Secretaries wanted to keep the Cabinet Secretariat happy since all their schemes and proposals passed through the Secretariat. Another reason was that the Chief Minister's approval was also required for these proposals. And so there was a direct line to the Chief Minister's office. At that time, Mrs Rabri Devi was Chief Minister.

The State Archives were in a mess. There were important manuscripts there as well as the State records. But they were not being stored properly and so were in danger of being destroyed. A scheme was launched to conserve and protect these records.

I came in as the Director of the State Education Project for three years and after that, I was the Chief Secretary of the Education Department for four years.

The condition of education in the State of Bihar was

deplorable. Since no teachers had been appointed for years, the majority of the schools were one- or two-teacher schools. In many villages the schools were conducted in the village courtyard, under a tree or in dilapidated buildings. The government schools did not open for even a hundred days in a year. The public had no faith in these schools. Private schools were springing up like mushrooms in the villages. Any young man who had passed his twelfth standard or got himself some kind of certification was putting up a board and opening an English-medium school. These schools had no basic structure and no trained teachers. And yet, the villagers would send their children to these schools because they were open for more than 300 days a year. The schools held prayers, they opened on time and closed at a fixed time. In addition, there were also tutors and tuition classes springing up in the villages. Even the poor would pay fifty or a hundred rupees to get their children additional coaching.

More than 12 per cent of Bihar's children were not in school. The number of girls enrolled was less than the number of boys. As there were not enough schools, the girls could not study after the eighth standard, and they were also being married off at a young age.

In 2005, Nitish Kumar came into power. Right in the beginning, his government decided that the highest priority would be given to good governance. The rule of law, which had all but collapsed, needed to be reinstated. The custodians of law and order were brought into a series of conferences and it was decided that important cases should be given priority and fast-tracked so that justice was not delayed and denied. In the past, cases would be filed but few would result in convictions and even these would take years. Now, the Patna High Court and the Police Headquarters began to monitor the investigation and trial of prominent cases, and a great change began to take place. Criminals realized that it was no longer easy to get away with crime in Bihar. The trials of some criminals with political connections began to be conducted in jail itself. The fear of kidnapping and ransom demands was also much reduced because a State-wide campaign was initiated to chase and arrest known offenders.

When Jharkhand became a separate State in 2000, the areas that were rich in mineral deposits and which had industries had all gone to the new State. Bihar was left with two-third of the original State's population but one-third of the land. It had to choose the path of progress while saddled with these challenges. Now that the State had few mineral resources, setting up traditional industries would be difficult. So the State chose to give priority to industries based on agriculture and both existing and potential intangible resources like education and cultural heritage.

Bihar had a huge pool of young people. If they were given a suitable education, they would find better jobs and their incomes would rise. Bihar's cultural heritage is among the richest in the country. Lord Buddha and Lord Mahavira had preached here and great rulers like Ashoka and Chandragupta Maurya had built their empires here. Ancient universities like Nalanda and Vikramshila had been founded here. And so, a decision was taken to highlight and enhance this cultural wealth and develop important tourist spots in the state.

Central to all of this, of course, was education. It was the Chief Minister's contention that development of the State would be impossible without a strong and consistent focus on education. As long as children were unlettered and innumerate, their economic condition could not improve. Every child should at least complete a school education. The problems were so many and so great that it was not possible to resolve all of them at once. The most important decision taken was that every child should be in school. To this end, a huge number of schools were started, existing schools had new rooms added to them, toilets were provided and teachers were hired. In order to restart the schools that had closed down, the teachers had to be brought back immediately. This could only happen if the local people were willing to be part of the endeavour.

It was decided that every village panchayat should have a Shiksha Mitra (Education Officer), chosen keeping in mind the reservation policies in force. Under the aegis of the Bihar Education Project around 80,000 Shiksha Mitras, both male and female, were hired at salaries of one thousand five hundred rupees per month. The decision was based on the belief that if the person were a local, they would not need close supervision; social pressure would be sufficient to make sure they would go to school every day. The result was that the closed government schools opened and began to function again. Later, their pay was also increased.

There was much debate on how teachers were to be selected.

It was found that choosing teachers in such large numbers was not possible at the State level. After a Constitutional amendment, the processes of education had been assigned to governments at the panchayat level. The government therefore decided that the selection of teachers would be the responsibility of the panchayat and civic bodies. Most of the training centres in Bihar were closed since there had been no trainers for many years. It was difficult to find them now. So, the Ministry of Education devised a proposal that the panchayats and civic bodies should hire teachers on a fixed pay scale. It was posited that one full-time regular teacher would be equal to the cost of three such teachers. This meant that the State government would not be put to any great additional expense. It was also decided that the selection should not involve an examination. Those who had passed the Intermediate examinations were considered to be qualified enough. Many young people who had passed this level were placed on a merit list while keeping reservations in mind.

A good thing was that half of the vacancies were reserved for women. The department was well aware that thousands of plans were being created and a very diverse population would be involved. There would be all kinds of debates. To ensure that the scheme should not end up in the courts, each district had an Appellate Authority which was constituted of a retired judicial officer and a government official. They were given the power to resolve any complaints that arose. Training the teachers was another huge challenge and so a correspondence course was started and the Indira Gandhi Open University was tasked with administering it. Later, training institutions were revived in the State.

It was also decided that there should be a primary school

within a kilometre of every child so that children would not have to walk too far to go to school. Thirty thousand new school buildings were built and one-and-a-half lakh new classrooms were added. Separate toilets were built for the boys and girls in every school. In order to train teachers, a training centre was opened in every block. Slowly the number of children out of school declined to below 1 per cent.

The number of girls enrolled was less than the number of boys. Often, a girl would not be enrolled because the family could not afford her uniform. The Balika Poshak Yojna (Girls Uniform Scheme) was started to provide uniforms and shoes for girls. This increased the number of girls in school and the sight of these girls in uniform on their way to school became an indicator of social change. Later, boys were also included in the uniform scheme.

The bicycle scheme is another important programme that brought about a great change in Bihar. Many States in the country have schemes under which Adivasi girl students are given cycles. Bihar had such a scheme as well. Once, Chief Minister Nitish Kumar was presenting cycles to Adivasi girls and at the end of the programme, over a hundred girls rode off confidently on their new cycles. The Chief Minister was deeply affected by the sight and its transformative power, and he decided that every ninth standard girl student in the State should get a bicycle. Many girls dropped out of school after the eighth standard because their families couldn't afford new uniforms, but mainly because higher secondary schools were situated in larger villages or towns and the girls would have to walk four or five kilometres to reach them. This meant that their parents often feared for their safety and did not send them to school. This was the problem the Chief Minister's new bicycle scheme sought to remedy. It was decided that any girl who passed the eighth standard and wanted to continue her studies should get a bicycle regardless of caste or community. This would raise their morale and reduce the time spent in travelling too. The families would also feel that their daughter had brought home a useful item.

Many people felt that all the girls should be given a particular type of cycle and the name of the Chief Minister's scheme should be inscribed on every cycle. It was their contention that if the girls' guardians were given money instead, they might not buy a good cycle, or not buy one at all. But the Chief Minister did not agree. I too was of the opinion that once the families received the money for the bicycles, the girls themselves would pressurize them to buy cycles of their own choice and if they chose one with an ISI mark, they could not go far wrong. And since they had exercised their choice, there was no question of the bicycle turning out to be a bad buy. Besides, government departments purchasing a large number of cycles would mean crores in taxes and the possibility of corruption as well.

When the scheme got underway, the scenes we witnessed were wonderful. Dozens of girls would set out together down the village paths on their bicycles and the way their faces lit up was a beautiful sight. The cycle freed up time for them to study and to do household work as well. Some people were of the opinion that girls on cycles would lay themselves open to wisecracks from men. As a result, another scheme was also launched to teach these girls martial arts.

We conducted a survey and found that 90 per cent of those who received money under the scheme had indeed bought the bicycles. In some cases, old cycles were modified, repaired and presented as new, but that was a negligible number. However, the scheme left the boys in schools feeling a bit jealous and noting this, the Chief Minister extended the scheme to boys as well after a few years.

During the pendency of this scheme, I was the Chief Secretary of the Education Department. We contacted the cycle companies and ensured they supplied cycles to wholesalers and retailers in sufficient numbers and at competitive rates. Seeing the size of the scheme, some of the big companies began setting up manufacturing units in Bihar. The success of this scheme was talked about not just at the national but also at the international level. The scheme received particular attention and praise at the London-based International Growth Centre (IGC) of the South Asia Growth Conference 2013. A research paper was presented here which stated that 98 per cent of those eligible had received the money and 90 per cent were happy with the scheme. In 2017, Kartik Muralidharan and Nitish Prakash published a research article titled 'Cycling to School: Increasing High School Enrolment for Girls in Bihar' in the *American Economy Journal*. In the same year, another important research paper titled 'Wheels of Power: Long-term Effects of Bihar Cycle Programme' co-authored by Shabana Mitra and O. Moine was also published.

Children were expected to work and earn money in poor households. The government wanted their parents to free them from this responsibility so that they might concentrate on studying and to this end, scholarships were instituted to encourage the students. Further, anyone who passed the tenth standard with a first class was given an award of ten thousand rupees.

To build so many new school buildings, to introduce lakhs of new classrooms, to build facilities for the schools, to create Block Resource Centres—this was no small task.

Hence, the government decided that this task should not be assigned to a single department for it would take too long. This responsibility was thus shifted to the school education committees which was composed of the parents of the students who studied in those schools. One reason for entrusting them with this task was that they would be building the schools in which their children would be studying and anyway, the villagers were in the habit of building their own four- and five-room homes. To give this project a brand identity, it was decided that all the schools should be painted the same colour so that anyone coming to the village should immediately see the schools and feel proud of them.

Building a school house was a complex process. The choice of location was the responsibility of the District Officer. Then the engineer presented a blue-print. This went to the District Officer who would give permission and the work would begin. There was a shortage of engineers at this level. Thus, there were many delays in the inspection, measuring and approvals. To ease this logjam, a scheme was devised to create five to six designs for the entire State, based on the availability of land. If there happened to be ample land, all the rooms could be on the ground floor. Where there wasn't, the school would have two storeys. The designs were devised to be earthquake-proof. All the designs were featured on a pamphlet and each School Education Committee was given the right to choose the design it thought would be appropriate. The problem of the shortage of engineers was handled too. A panel of engineers was created at the block level. The school committees were given the right to choose an engineer from the panel to get the work done. A budgetary allocation of 2 per cent was made for this.

All these innovations meant that school buildings of good quality came up in many villages over the next three or four years. Their total cost came up to four to five thousand crores. Every panchayat now had a shop selling construction materials like bricks, sand, cement and steel rods; many people also found employment. A great wave of excitement spread through the whole State. There came a time when 20 per cent of the State budget was being spent on education.

A survey of Patna's government schools demonstrated how much talent was to be found among these marginalised and underprivileged children, many of whom lived in slums. Their talents had to be drawn out but the lives of these children were hemmed in by the daily struggle for survival. But this only strengthened their desire to learn new things. It occurred to me that we needed to start a meaningful project to develop their talents. And this was the beginning of the Kilkari organization.

'Kilkari' was my dream project. It had taken root when I was the District Development officer in Dumka. At that time, there was a scheme to bring children who were ragpickers or working as domestic servants to school. The government started Shramik schools for them. The children got free text books and notebooks as well as a mid-day meal. They also received a hundred rupees every month, which was meant to cover the earnings they or their families would lose now that they were in school. I was supposed to go and inaugurate one of the first of these schools in Jamtara, Dumka. On the way there, I kept wondering how children from such backgrounds could be made to stay in school. How could the importance of education be explained to them? Would they understand what I had to say? But when I arrived at the school I was in for a huge surprise. It was, in fact, an education for me.

The children there were much brighter and had much more experience than children who had advantages that they had never had. These children had lived on the streets in extremely difficult conditions and had faced many tough situations in their young lives, yet, retained the ability to smile. They were much more knowledgeable than their age suggested. In this way, they were far ahead of children from ordinary families. That day, I thought that if these children were allowed to develop their talents as they wished, the results could be extraordinary under the right guidance. This was where the idea of Kilkari was born. There were two guiding principles: there would be no formal education here and the children would learn only what they wanted to and what they were interested in. For instance, if a child wanted to study folk music, she would not be forced to study classical music. The children would choose their field and the best minds in that field would be on hand to train them. The nation's best artists, painters, musicians, theatre persons, photographers and scientists were invited to interact with the children and execute projects with them.

Children from this programme have gone on to win national and international awards in cinema, photography, theatre and other art forms. Dozens of these children have gone to work in Mumbai's film world as child actors. They take part in theatre at the national level as well. Some have been awarded patents for their inventions.

The building of this organization, too, was conceived along the principles of Building as Learning Aid (BALA). A huge playground would welcome the children. Many of the walls of the building were blackboards where children could write or draw or work out mathematical problems. Different types of trees and saplings were planted around the building and a playground with swings was set up.

Most of the children came from underprivileged families and were between the ages of eight to sixteen. My wife was of the opinion that the savings habit should be inculcated in them and that they should learn to keep accounts. And so, the Kilkari Children's Bank was started. Children deposited five to ten rupees and could withdraw it when they needed it. They even earned interest on the money.

The responsibility of running the bank was also given to the children. The children chose a manager among themselves and over time, lakhs of rupees accumulated in the bank. But the real success was that poor children found a cheerful, enabling atmosphere here. It was a place where they could feel free and so it became a really popular spot. The children who had trained at Kilkari began to find work in films. They won national-level awards and also travelled outside the State. Using the library and the computer room at Kilkari, some children got admission at the Indian

Institute of Technology (IIT). The organization became a role model in Bihar.

The atmosphere in the Bihar Education Project was a very different one. There were no assistants and no principal assistant; work was done in teams. Each important issue had its own Chief Officer. Each officer kept their files with them.

When I joined, I tried some experiments. The first was to have a weekly meeting on Monday in which all the officers would join in to make decisions. This had the advantage that all the officers were now aware of what was going on in other departments even if the decisions taken had no real connection with their sections. The other benefit was that the officers had to give their feedback and opinions on all the decisions that were taken. For instance, if the Education department was proposing to build new toilets for schools, the Gender Coordinator might have suggestions about the girls' toilets—that they should be airy and should be provided with windows—even if this meant spending a little more money.

To increase their feelings of ownership in the programmes, we removed all restrictions of timings—the officers could come and go as they pleased.

I had noticed that many officers would stay in the office till late at night, but not get their work done. They needed to work during the day and go home at night. Earlier, tea would be served only twice, in the morning and in the evening. Now tea was made available at all hours. And it was made mandatory that visitors should at least be offered a cup of tea and a glass of water. All the officers were given data cards for their mobiles to facilitate communication. At that time, this was unheard of. In the beginning, everyone was delighted. Later, they began to feel they were always on call.

There was an honest and hard-working officer of the Bihar Education Scheme who did not have a good rapport with his colleagues. He had a contrarian approach to things. I could not find a way to get him to work in a happy fashion. One day, when I was at a programme for disabled children, I saw that he seemed to be taking a great deal of interest in the children. Later, I put him in charge of a department dealing with such children. He worked diligently, taking decisions with such speed that the programmes created for the disabled children in the Bihar Education Project began to gather momentum and within a couple of years, they were considered among the best. Afterwards, we discovered that he had a child who was disabled.

There was a Directorate of Public Education but it was moribund. In the decade after the year 2000, literacy campaigns had been successfully run in various districts of Bihar. For a variety of reasons, these had been abandoned. Nor was literacy one of the government's priorities. The main reason for this was that the problem of illiteracy had been contained to a few Hindi-speaking districts. Bihar had one of the lowest rates of literacy in the country. Half of the population was illiterate and one-third of the women could neither read nor write. I believed that as long as this continued, Bihar would never be able to progress. It was important to improve female literacy. The new government's priority was the upliftment of women.

A decision was taken to run a programme called Akshar Aanchal. The first meeting took place in the A.N. Sinha Institute and the Chief Minister participated in it.

I had been invited to other States to share my experiences with literacy campaigns in Bihar.

This meant I had some experience of the situation in other states. A committee was put together in the State Education Project which brought together all those who had some expertise in the field of literacy. We needed a huge army of volunteers and these had to be trained as well. Before the scheme was rolled out, we made a huge attempt to affect a change in the environment. Hundreds of literacy songs were written and plays devised, and across a million walls, slogans were painted, and people's representatives were called to meetings. These initiatives were focused on the districts. Each district had its own Art Initiative. This work was carried out in high style across the State.

The initiatives of giving female students cycles and clothes was now paying off. Their status had improved and they participated in the literacy campaign with enthusiasm and energy. The goals of the drive were kept simple and focused. Besides learning the three 'r's of reading, writing and 'rithmetic, they were also made aware of the schemes and initiatives of the government. A pamphlet outlining those government schemes designed to benefit women and children was written in simple language, printed and distributed. Whenever the Chief Minister went on tour, he made it a point to visit the office of the Literacy Campaign and in every speech, he would urge his audiences to send their children to school.

In some districts this scheme ran for two years; in others, for three. As a result, Bihar's rate of literacy rose from 47 per cent to 62 per cent. Among women, the literacy rate was 33 per cent and it went up to 52 per cent. Bihar won the Best Improvement in Literacy and in Female Literacy award in 2011. I received both these awards from the President in New Delhi. It was a day that warmed my heart.

I was posted several times to the Art, Culture and Youth department of the Bihar government. Perhaps the powers that be had some inkling of my interest in arts and sports. When I was first posted to this department in 1996 as Special Secretary-cum-Director, the budget was about 5 crores. During my postings there, Bihar hosted many international and national events. The Asian School Games Football Tournament was held. Many state-wide cultural events were held in Patna's Gandhi Maidan in style. A National Youth Festival was started and the Moin-ul-Haq Stadium acquired a sports academy.

The Central government chose Bihar to host the Youth Festival in 2006. The Bihar government was not sure whether it could pull it off. At that time, I was the Principal Secretary of the Art, Culture and Youth department. After the new government was sworn in, the Chief Minister called me in and asked if we could manage to organize it in a month. I said we certainly could.

Organizing a National Youth Festival is perceived as a huge task. More than 5,000 participants from across the country take part in it. We took this on as a challenge and decided to hold the event on 12 January, Swami Vivekananda's birthday. There were very few good hotels in Bihar. This meant that accommodating more than 5,000 people was going to be a problem. There were not enough auditoria for all the planned events. Despite these hurdles, we decided to hold the event, relying mainly on the enthusiasm of the people of Bihar, especially the youth.

One hundred young persons from Bihar were chosen and trained as liaisons with the teams from various States. We had a meeting with the hotel owners and they were instructed on improving their rooms and bathrooms. They were given to understand that this was an important moment for 'Brand Bihar' and we were all going to have to put our shoulders to the wheel.

Providing good food for such a large number of people for a week was also a huge challenge. Special arrangements were made for this in the courtyard of the Golghar under the supervision of the then Chief Secretary G.S. Kang. All the auditoria and surroundings were decorated by artists from Bihar. The whole festival went off with a bang and with no misadventures. All our guests were pleased with the hospitality of Bihar. Any shortfall in basic infrastructure was compensated for by the warmth of the people. In later editions of the festival, Bihar 2006 was still talked about.

At that time, arranging an international tournament was a big challenge for Bihar. But we still decided to organize the Asian Football Tournament in which fourteen nations participated. We did not have five-star hotels in which to put them up. There was a lack of good sports fields as well. We had to refurbish the Moin-ul-Haq Stadium and those at Patna Science College and Patna College. The Mithilesh Stadium, Danapur was in a dilapidated state. Rooms in the good hotels were given a make-over and excellent food was organized. English-speaking youth were identified and assigned to the teams as guides. Patna was a city electrified by the festival. The players and officials who had come from various countries were impressed by the warmth and hospitality of the people of Bihar. And as a result of this, when the next edition was held in South Korea, the Sports Minister and I were invited as guests.

The cultural programmes held at Gandhi Maidan were also unparalleled. A large number of artists from different districts participated. The entire programme lasted for three days with huge audiences watching them until late in the night. Four or five stages had been built in Gandhi Maidan on which music programmes were held. Earthen walls were erected and paintings by Bihar's artists were exhibited on them. All the participating artists were honoured. This was the first time so many artists had come together at Gandhi Maidan. The programme was remembered for a long time afterwards.

When I was posted as the Special Secretary-cum-Director of the Art, Culture and Youth department, the Departmental Secretary was very happy about the organization of these programmes. People said they had never seen him look that cheerful. But he took a great deal of time to make decisions on files. And he found it difficult to come to a decision about them. This made things tough because these programmes occasioned many expenses and payments had to be made immediately. I found a way out of this by presenting the file to him at the sports ground or at the performance spot itself. Once, when I was getting a bill for breakfast approved, he remarked that it was a rather large amount. I said that we had to feed all the participants and give them tea as well. I also pointed out that the breakfast was the same one that he had enjoyed as was the tea. It was only then that the requisition was sanctioned!

The departmental Minister would be present with me at the programme venues and the sports fields. The Secretary had marked the Minister on many files that were not strictly necessary. However, the Minister would okay them quickly. Later, the Honourable Secretary went about saying that I had often compelled him to sign off on files, which was true to some extent. But without doing this, the show could not have gone on—especially big shows like the one at Gandhi Maidan.

I was also the Agricultural Production Commissioner for a short time.

Bihar is primarily an agriculture economy. The land is fertile, the farmers are hardworking and they waste no time in adopting new techniques. A good example of this came up when I took the Nobel-winning economist Professor Joseph E. Stiglitz to see organic farming in the state. A farmer had planted two plots with cauliflower. He told

Professor Stiglitz that one of them was organic and he was proud of the quality of the produce. The second plot had been cultivated with chemical fertilizers. Professor Stiglitz was surprised to discover that both plots belonged to the same farmer. If the farmer knew how good the quality of the crop reared by organic methods was, why hadn't he used the same method on both the plots? The farmer replied that he wanted to see the results for himself and so he had used chemical fertilizers as a control test. Professor Stiglitz was delighted at this reply and said that the farmers of Bihar were as good, if not better, than scientists.

Bihar grows fruit and vegetables on a large scale, and it leads the country in the production of honey. It is a State where three crops of cabbage are grown each year and two of corn. Many farmers have become prosperous by planting corn; the government has supported them, but they took the initiative themselves. The problem with agriculture in Bihar is not one of productivity. Instead, it is one of preservation, packaging and protection from middlemen.

I had only been at the Agriculture department for a short while when the then Chief Minister, Nitish Kumar, asked me to take charge of all the departments. In August 2012, I became Secretary. The Chief Minister's Secretariat worked all hours. If there had been an untoward incident of any kind in the state, our day would begin at 8 a.m. and would often continue until late at night. Generally, however, the Secretariat functioned from 10 a.m. to 8 p.m. But then the Chief Minister was also hard at work throughout the day. If there was tension in any region, he would speak directly to the officials concerned and was always available for making important decisions.

Working in the Chief Minister's office gave me an opportunity to get to know Nitish Kumar better. His life was orderly and his work was systematic and punctual. He had a simple lifestyle and he was disciplined in his speech and habits. I never saw him in a rage and I never heard him address anyone else as 'tum' (or with disrespect). He was a glutton for work. One of the best examples of this was the 'Janta ke Darbar mein Mukhyamantri' (The Chief Minister in the Court of the People). Thousands of people would come to present their problems at this forum. There were times when those issues seemed to reflect only a desire for personal gain or were quite simply illegal. I would often feel angry but the Chief Minister listened quietly.

There were other instances in which a team from the Chief Minister's Secretariat would be dispatched on the same day to intervene and resolve the issue. A record was kept of all these requests to make follow-up easy. Often this programme would begin in the morning and continue up to 6 or 7 p.m. To keep people warm, bonfires were lit and tea was provided.

Almost every year, the Chief Minister would go on a yatra, each one with a different name. There was the Nyaay Yatra (Justice Pilgrimage) and the Vikaas Yatra (Progress Procession). The routine there was even more demanding. We would visit the various projects on the ground and then the Chief Minister would meet local representatives of the people to hear their opinions and solutions. For some inexplicable reason, these journeys always took place in the hottest or the coldest seasons. It was clear that the Chief Minister preferred to go out among the people, to survey

Bihar, to understand its problems and to oversee projects rather than staying in Patna.

The CM was a strict vegetarian, and his food had to be made with as little oil and spices as possible. I was the exact opposite—a committed non-vegetarian who ate fish almost every day. During my time as Chief Secretary, I ate hundreds of meals with the Chief Minister and discovered that dal and veggies could be tasty too. When the day had gone well, egg bhujiya or Bihari bachka were on the menu. My tastes changed and I began to appreciate the joys of vegetarian food.

A political leader has a fixed term of office: five years. And he/she must show maximum results during this time, before going back to the people in the hope of another term. When I was in the Education department as Principal Secretary, I observed that once the Chief Minister had decided on a scheme, it took, on an average, a week for it to be given final shape and okayed by the cabinet of ministers. Whether it was a scheme for school uniforms, cycles or scholarships, it was then cleared by the Finance Department and the Planning Commission, too, in about a week and was implemented soon after. At the Centre, I had seen that it took a year for a scheme to go from conception to approval and implementation.

The Bihar CM was a man in a hurry. However, the work culture in Bihar was not conducive to speed. The polity had been divided on the lines of caste and religion and it was difficult to win anyone's trust. And so, whatever schemes were created were kept open to all; none were devised for those of a particular caste or creed. This led people to feel that the government was concerned about all of them.

I had never met someone like Nitish Kumar. Here was a man who had total control over his life. He did not believe in breaking or circumventing any law. He believed that if we wanted to get things done quickly, we should ignore those pettifogging laws that got in the way of doing things in the people's best interests. The Chief Minister's stand was that if a law was obstructive, it should be changed. Even though this might be an arduous process, he believed that it was better to go through all the steps, however, time-consuming they may be.

In 2014, I became the Chief Secretary of State. As Secretary General of the Chief Minister's Secretariat, I had had some experience of the many departments of the government and so the transition was not difficult. I knew the priorities of most departments, what projects were on going and where intense monitoring was needed.

I had also noted how much time Chief Secretaries spent in meetings. Some spent the entire day in meetings and these often ran into the night too. The number of meetings increased because departments were reluctant to make decisions at their level and kicked them upstairs. I did not approve of wasting time on tea and snacks and personal anecdotes. In the first week, I announced that the first few days would be free of meetings so that the Departmental Secretaries could get on with their work. These Secretaries had multiple calls on their schedule as they had to attend meetings with the Chief Minister, ministers of their department and the Chief Secretary, and at the Vidhan Sabha and Vidhan Parishad. In addition, there was the High Court. All this meant that they could rarely find the time to attend to the work for which they were responsible. The meeting-free days allowed them to make time to attend to their own work. These days could also be used to conduct surveys of the State.

During my tenure, it was necessary to explain why a meeting was necessary before it was called. If the issue only affected the department, they could discuss the file with me for my inputs. If it concerned two or more departments, then only those Secretaries were called. Each department had to indicate clearly what the issue at hand was and what was expected of me. This meant that people began to take decisions at their own levels and fewer issues were brought to my notice.

Furthermore, I tried to ensure that no meeting should run for more than an hour. Opinions had to be concise and clear. No stories, no snacks. This meant that many meetings could be completed in a day. It often happened that a Secretary might turn up ten minutes late for a meeting only to find that it was over. Whoever conducted departmental meetings had to have a format. Whatever important amendments had to be made would be made, and on the same day, the signed documents would be returned to the relevant departments and concerned officers. In this way, much time was saved.

In the matter of leave, I was of the opinion that the good workers would not ask for leave unless there was some real reason and as for those who took leave regularly, it did not matter much whether they were in office or not. There was no shortage of good officers in the Bihar cadre. I can say there were many who surpassed me in conscientiousness and efficiency. As far as it was possible, I listened to the officers' problems and tried to find solutions. I did not believe that they should work late into the night. I often said that there wasn't that much work if it were done right. Through my entire career, I had never found myself short on time or on resources for good work. And despite the fact that I worked in a poor State like Bihar, I advised my officers never to work in or create an atmosphere of tension. If you work happily, the work goes quickly and well. Of course, I knew that we were never going to solve all the problems at hand. Some we would have to leave to Father Time and Mother Nature.

Every year, Bihar faced some natural disaster or the other. It was entirely possible for a flood and a drought to strike the State at the same time. Since Bihar's was basically an agrarian economy, it fell to the government to step up and help farmers when their crops failed. The Chief Minister believed that those affected by disasters had first call on the State's Treasury. And so, priority was given to the schemes that were devised to help them.

The Chief Minister spearheaded all emergency relief measures for those affected by the disaster and paid special attention to the arrangements made for their resettlement and care. Once when a dam on the River Kosi broke and caused a flood, he sent all the Secretaries of all the departments to the area. The flood-affected people were settled in huge tents constructed around the university and other high schools. Some among them were given the task of cleaning and others were chosen to cook. Temporary schools were set up for the children along with aanganwadis, and arrangements were made for pregnant women to deliver safely. Every morning, the children were brought together to do a drill, to exercise and study. Many observers came from other States to study the arrangements that had been made for the flood-affected.

Bihar's development model was also different from that of other States. Since it is a rural economy of villages and farming, the rural poor were the focus of development.

The ways Bihar has chosen to deal with Naxalism are different from those used in the rest of the country. In many States, they are only seen as terrorists and opponents of progress of the States. It is true that Naxal leaders try to bring the poor into their field and manipulate them in order to grow their sphere of influence. They blow up bridges or destroy roads, ambush government vehicles and mount attacks on police stations to loot weapons. And they levy 'taxes' on traders and contractors in the areas under their influence. The government response in most States and by the Centre has been a policy of extermination of the Naxals and driving them out of the areas they control. In Bihar, the attitude is that the Naxal is a citizen who has gone astray and has been brainwashed. It is true that there are violent elements, but most are regular citizens. If good programmes of development are started in the affected areas and employment opportunities are provided, the problems will sort themselves out. There must also be a political attempt to bring them into the mainstream. They must be connected to development programmes.

In Bihar, because of this approach, many people branded as Naxals began to participate in panchayat elections and became representatives of the people. The State government started programmes like 'Aapki Sarkar, Aapki Dwaar' (Your Government, Your Doorway) for Naxal-affected areas which gave priority to development. Centres to impart vocational training were opened there too. It was my experience that Naxal leaders would enlist poor Adivasis or Scheduled Caste youths who had not finished their education, so, attempts were made to give them a chance to reform instead of trying to kill them. The police were told that if they heard of any attempts at sabotage or if there were any attacks on government property, they should respond with the full force of the law. But the Naxals involved must be caught and given appropriate punishment. The police were not given carte blanche to fire at them without reason or to unduly spread terror.

It was also my experience during my time at the Ministry of Education that Naxals would rarely attack public property such as schools. Once, when a school in Gaya was bombed, I called the leaders and told them that the schools had been set up for the poor. What could be the rationale for bombing them? Their answer was amazing; they had only bombed three-storey structures that were, in fact, not schools but buildings where the police had set up camps to disrupt their activities. When I looked into the matter, I found the claim to be true. I brought the leaders up to date with the Literacy Campaign that the government was running. They asked me what the slogans for the campaign were and said they would paint them on the walls of the villages. They did keep their word.

Once, a high-level conference on the Naxal movement

was called, and the governments of Chhattisgarh, Jharkhand, Bihar, Andhra Pradesh and Odisha sent Chief secretaries and DGPs for the conference. I was the Chief Secretary of the State then. For a long time, the discussion focused on how to fight the Naxals by increasing the weaponry and raising budgetary allocations. Eventually, I got angry and said that this was not right. These were after all citizens of our country who had lost their way and it was the government's job to bring them back into the mainstream. Spending more on weapons would not bring a resolution; increasing employment opportunities in these areas would. If the aim was to merely to kill all the Naxalites, it would make more economic sense to hire an international organization to systematically go after them and exterminate them. This would not only be cheaper; it would probably take only two or three months to do the job. The other participants in the meeting were astonished. However, they did not seem to have any real answers either. They ended the meeting by saying that different people have different views on how to deal with the Naxalites.

At one point in time, Bihar was held to be second to none in terms of local self-government. Paul Appleby, a theorist of public administration, had once conducted a survey of India's administration. In his study, Bihar stood first in administration and legislation. But over time as the other States began to contend with the Centre to work out their own destinies and as they began to pass laws, Bihar slowly turned into a hotbed of economic inequality and communal strife.

Since Independence, Bihar, located in the heart of the

Hindi belt, had always cooperated with the government at the Centre. Unlike other States such as Punjab, Assam or the southern States, Bihar never put any pressure on the Central government to further its development. But the fact is that although many parliamentarians have been elected from here, the policies of the Central government have not been favourable to Bihar. Although Bihar was rich in mineral wealth, for example, the Centre's freight equalization policy meant that it derived no benefit from this.

There were other disadvantages. Bihar was a feudal State with power concentrated in the hands of the upper castes. Ninety per cent of the land was held by 10 per cent of the population and so, land resources could not be optimized. In the last fifty years, few factories or industries have come up in the State, and Bihar has remained basically an agrarian State. Biharis go outside the State to find work. After 1990, under the dispensations that came to power in the State, the situation worsened. It is true that there was an awakening among the lower castes and that the hegemony of the upper castes was weakened, but the economy was devastated. Crime increased, kidnapping was common and since there was little employment, migration out of the State increased. The health and education systems were in shambles. For a long time, no appointments had been made in universities and colleges, resulting in a decline in the quality of education. A shortage of doctors meant that government hospitals could not function efficiently. Farmers were not getting a fair price for their produce as they could not take it to the market.

Things got worse when Jharkhand became an

independent State. Bihar was a feudal society. Even the rich were investing their money in other cities. The law-and-order situation was abysmal. The roads were cratered with potholes and so it took hours to traverse short distances. A miasma of despair hung over the State government officials. They were petrified into inaction. All they wanted was to do as little as possible and save their jobs. Politics was the playground of thugs and goondas. Most of the officers from Bihar were trying to get posted to other States and were buying land or flats in other metropolises so they might retire there and benefit from better infrastructure.

It was against this background that my friends and I began to look for suitable land near Delhi when I was posted at the Centre. We planned to settle there after retirement. We found some suitable land about forty kilometres from Delhi in the Gautam Buddha Nagar district near the Dadri Thermal Plant. This was on the eastern Ganga canal. About thirty-five to forty of us put in two lakhs each and bought 1000 gaz (one gaz is equivalent to nine square feet). The idea was to build a village there after retirement and live together, close to the people one knew. Among these, we included police officer, businessmen, MLAs, farmers and others; many castes and creeds were also represented. It was a pleasant area to live in and not too far from Delhi. I wanted to open a nursery for plants there.

But in 2005, things changed. At the end of that year, a new government was voted in. Progress started to happen at a rapid pace. The law-and-order situation improved and basic infrastructure began to be strengthened. Biharis and those from outside the State began to invest in Bihar. The electric supply improved dramatically. A network of roads sprang up, connecting the villages. As a result, the idea of living in a village near Delhi post-retirement was put on the back burner. Most of my friends now see that land as an investment.

When Jharkhand became an independent State, Bihar could only rely on education, agri-based industries and tourism as progress routes. A plan was devised to present Bihar as a soft State. It was necessary to create the right image of Bihar at the national and international levels so that its ancient and venerable history, art and culture should be made widely known. Although Patna had a beautiful museum and there were local museums in the districts, they were not well-maintained nor were their treasures of world-renowned art displayed to their best advantage. The Patna Museum did not even have enough room to display its treasures. A proposal was made to construct two new galleries to exhibit these treasures.

While on a tour of the Patna Museum, the Chief Minister said that the display and showcasing of the objects should match their beauty and importance. For this, a grand new museum would be needed where these could be displayed as they might be showcased anywhere in the developed world. And the Patna Museum would be simultaneously renovated and brought up to international standards. Together, both these museums would present a holistic picture of the heritage, culture and history of Bihar.

Bihar was blessed with great cultural and artistic wealth which was not being presented properly at the Patna Museum. Its most famous exhibit was the Didarganj Yakshi, whose beauty has been praised for long not just across India but around the world. The story of its discovery is a strange one. It was lying on the banks of the Ganga in Patna for years. Dhobis would beat clothes on it. One day, some children in the area saw a snake under the stone structure and turned it over to find that it was, in fact, a life-size sculpture of a woman. It was then brought to the museum and went on to earn worldwide fame. The Bihar Museum also has some beautiful terracotta figures whose hair is beautifully adorned. The other famous sculptures found during excavations in Bihar include that of a laughing boy and girl. The Kurkihar Bronzes of the Patna Museum are also world famous. They are named after the area in which they were found. There are also many Hindu deities and figures of Lord Buddha made of stone and metal—all proof of how advanced Bihar's art forms were in ancient times.

In the heart of Patna, five ministerial residences that stood by the Patna High court were cleared and fourteen acres of land were made available. It was decided that cultural artefacts from pre-historic times up to 1740 CE should be brought to the new museum and the rest would remain in the Patna Museum. Exhibits in these two museums would thus give visitors a good understanding of Bihar's history. The two museums would be linked by a tunnel, which would also be decorated with art and artifacts.

To build a new museum of international standards is a

huge challenge because most of the museums in India either house the personal collections of royalty or else were built by the British. There are only a few private museums and they tend to be quite small. Indian culture, heritage and art is now famous across the world but neither the Centre nor the States have considered it worthwhile to create a modern museum after Independence.

Against this backdrop, it was obvious that in order to set up a museum of international standard, it would be necessary to study some international museums. It would also be imperative to choose an organization that had some experience in setting up such museums. The well-known Lord Cultural Resources, Canada, was chosen as our conceptual consultant. I was the Chief Secretary of the Education Department then but was still chosen as the Nodal Officer of the Museum Project. The order also stated that whatever post I was moved to, this project would remain with me.

When the idea of the Bihar Museum was floated and land was being acquired for it, some of Patna's intellectuals and economists raised objections. They contended that as a poor State Bihar should not be spending 500 crores on a museum. This money could be used for roads, schools and other infrastructure or even to develop other older, well-established museums and important cultural sites. We did not think this was a valid argument as the government had already made education and health a priority, and there were plans in place to improve existing facilities as tourist attractions. We were certain of the need for an ambitious project that would restore Bihar's faith and pride in its culture and showcase the State's rich history for a younger generation.

But not everyone was convinced and many lawsuits were filed in the Patna High Court which took years to settle. I argued in the High Court that it was the prerogative of the democratically-elected government to choose the path of progress for its State.

The Bihar Museum was to be built according to international standards of museology, and Lord's Resources were made the master plan consultants. National and international architects were invited to send across plans for the new building. An international jury was set up to decide who should be awarded the contract. Martin Roth, director Victoria and Albert Museum; Ms Róisín Heneghan from Ireland; Subhodh Gupta, an internationally recognized artist of Bihari origin; Neelkanth Chhaya, Dean, School of Architecture, Ahemedabad; and Tanmay Tathagat of Environmental Solutions were among the jury.

Of the five firms that were shortlisted, Fosters of London scored the highest points on technique. But when technique and economics were considered together, Maki and Associates of Japan led the field. The designs that were sent in were all amazing and came from world-renowned architects. Fosters, which had designed the great court for the British Museum, submitted a design that was futuristic in the extreme. The roof looked like an immense egg tray. This design scored high on technique, but my contention was that in order to enjoy the roof, viewers would have to hire a helicopter! There were no tall buildings in the immediate vicinity from which the roof might be viewed. Maki's design, on the other hand, evoked memories of Nalanda. And it took into account the surroundings; the building envisaged would not tower above the street and we felt that its low-slung shape would be welcoming to visitors. The simplicity of the design also appealed to us. It also addressed one of Patna's long-standing problems: noise pollution. The seven courtyards in the design immediately created an atmosphere of quiet and serenity. Unlike most modern buildings, this one would not be enclosed and air-conditioned; instead, it made good use of natural light and air to ventilate it. When the designs had been approved by the committee, we placed the shortlisted ones before the Chief Minister and he found Maki's beautiful and attractive.

From the survey of modern museums, it became clear that museology had come a long way. It would no longer do to simply put up some statues and a few artworks. The museum of today must present the past of the State but it must also showcase the contemporary artwork of modern and folk artists. The museum must look to the past, engage with the present and anticipate the future. It is important that it engages with children and the youth. We decided that the restaurants in the complex must serve Bihari food. The museum also had to serve as a cultural centre. It was decided that the restaurant, museum shop, auditorium and international convention centre should remain open until 10 p.m. so that a variety of programmes—ranging from music and theatre to literature—could take place. This would turn it into a new cultural hub for the city.

The construction was assigned to Larsen & Toubro. The design was relatable and inviting. It would beautify the city in which it would stand. The idea was not to build an impersonal skyscraper but to create a venue that would look new and interesting but which would not intimidate people. Maki and Associates also took on the responsibility of presenting the artefacts within the museum to their best advantage. They made no compromises in this or any other matter, even if it meant taking more time over the detailing. The total budget was 500 crores, of which 300 crores was spent on the building and 200 on the interiors and facilities. The interior design was handled by an international company based in Singapore which had worked with many museums before.

When work began, some people filed a case in the

Patna High Court, claiming that a 500-crore budget might be better used on infrastructure, education and other cultural institutions. Although the High Court declined to stop the project, it did pass strictures on the expenditure of public money on the project. Our contention was that infrastructure and education were important and they were being attended to but a modern, world-class museum was as much a necessity as these.

When the Bihar Museum opened its doors, it was an international success. It won two national awards for design: The *India Today* Award and the Centre of International Modern Art (CIMA) Award. At the international level, it was selected for the If Design Award in international branding and corporate communications in February 2018. It is now a symbol of Bihar, identified with the State. It attracts more than a thousand visitors a day. In order to ensure that people keep coming back, a variety of events such as art camps, exhibitions, lectures and music programmes are held here regularly.

The success of the project led to many other States thinking that they might benefit from setting up a modern museum as well. A number of representations came to Patna to see how this might be achieved.

Before we started the project, I was given the opportunity to visit some of the important museums of the world. Our concept consultant, Lord Cultural Resources, collaborated with us on this. And so, I was able to meet the directors and curators of many world-class institutions. This was an education in itself. There were many questions to be answered: why has the footfall been declining? Is a museum really essential in our modern age? Why are so many museums facing a financial crunch? How can a museum be turned into a vibrant cultural space? How can it be made a major tourist attraction?

I began my tour of the museums in New York where I visited the Metropolitan Museum, the Museum of Modern Art and the Guggenheim. In Paris, I saw the Louvre, the Pompidou Centre, the Musée d'Orsay and some other museums. In San Francisco, I visited the San Francisco Museum of Modern Art, the Asian Art Museum and the Museum of African Diaspora, among others. In Japan, I went to the Tokyo National Museum, the National Museum of Tokyo, the Hiroshima Peace Museum and the Nara Museum. In Great Britain, my list included the British Museum, the Victoria & Albert Museum, the Tate and the National Gallery. These were a revelation, not just in terms of the beauties of the exhibits, but in the philosophy behind the exhibits and events.

None of the museums above are merely a collection of objects. They are all centres of art for their cities, their countries and the entire world. Their calendar is full of art-and-culture-related events. The exhibits keep changing. They have exchange programmes with other museums. Most museums pay special attention to the young and to children. Education and research are special areas of interest. Various means are used to make the museum experience enjoyable for visitors. Care is taken to ensure that people with special needs should face no difficulty in visiting and viewing the exhibits. Some museums are so popular that the income from ticket sales is enough to cover operating costs. The

Louvre in Paris gets lakhs of visitors. Bilbao in Spain was going through an economic recession but the opening of a new museum brought about a turnaround and a rise in the number of tourists.

The museum of today seeks to provide an immersive experience for the visitor. Some people want to view the art, others want to conduct research. Some want to explore the gift shop while still others would like to have a meal. There are those who have come for the exhibitions. Others are attracted to the cultural conversations that happen there.

In India, my experience has been that special exhibitions last for one or two weeks. There is a fixed lighting system which does not respond to the needs of the different works on display. In the international museums, the exhibition spaces are vast and each exhibition is mounted with care. The colours of the walls may change to suit the exhibits; the lighting certainly does. Each exhibition lasts for three or four months so that people may visit them at their leisure. They are often so popular that you have to book tickets in advance and people do.

How the exhibits should be displayed is decided with the help of experts and with great attention to detail.

What the visitor's experience should be like is decided well in advance. Only then are the artefacts displayed. I was astonished to see that when the artefact was made of paper or textiles, subtle and diffused lighting was used in preference to direct light. This is to preserve both the dyes and inks and the material itself. Special lighting is often used to highlight certain aspects of an item on display. Audio guides, sound effects and various apps are all made available to help enhance the visitor experience. Docents or guides may be specially trained for an exhibition.

Another thing that surprised me was that items made of cloth or paper were not displayed for more than six months. After this, they are allowed to 'rest' for six months in the dark. All the objects are regularly inspected for wear and tear. Conservation and restoration experts are on hand to help ameliorate the effects of the passage of time. In many developed nations, museums receive assistance from corporate houses but they are always independently managed. Everything we learned at these museums was put to use in creating a world-class museum in Bihar.

There is no tradition of public art in Bihar. At the most, you will find a statue of a political leader at some crossroad. This was not the case in the big metropolises of the West. Paris, London and New York abound in modern art in public places. Many streets are decked with graffiti which they refer to as 'street art'; the citizens of these countries enjoy freedom of self-expression and make their views known in this manner. Many of these are anonymous, completed in secret.

I thought it might be a good idea to install eye-catching pieces of art in public places. We were in the process of turning a filthy stream that flowed past the Secretariat into a beautiful park and we had decided to install four or five artworks there. I wanted to commission the very best artists. It was in this connection that I got in touch with the Bihar-born and internationally-renowned artist Subodh Gupta. His work had also been acquired by several museums. His sculptures sold at prices of around 2 and 4 crores.

While speaking to him, I made the point that being in a collection of a private individual was one thing but it was quite another for one to be on public display. I pointed out that while he was well-known on the world art scene, few people knew of him in Bihar which was where he had been born. I confessed that the government would not be able to match his international prices. But I also pointed out that hundreds of thousand ordinary people would be taking selfies with his work and it would thus acquire a new digital life in another sphere. Considering his international price however, I decided to earmark 1 crore rupees for the project. The next step was to get this amount—for a work of art—approved!

This has always been a problem in acquiring a work of art or paying an artist for a performance. We constituted a committee, of which I was the Chairman, that was tasked with considering the record of prices paid for his work. We fixed on the sum of 1 crore rupees. Such committees then became the norm in matters of making payments in the Art, Culture and Youth department. In the Rajdhani Vatika—as this garden was named, there is an artwork by Subodh Gupta, one by Rajat Ghosh and an installation called Nalanda Relic by Diane Hagen and Sanjiv Sinha. Rajat Ghosh and Sanjiv Sinha got 18 lakhs each; Diane Hagen, 10 lakhs. Other than Hagen, all the artists had roots in Bihar. All this came out of the budget for the centenary celebrations of Bihar Day. I had commissioned two artworks from Sanjiv Sinha and Diane Hagen for the Buddha Enlightened programme at Bodh Gaya and afterwards, I brought them to the Vatika. Other artworks went to the Gandhi Museum and other institutions.

When the Vatika was inaugurated, the *Times of India* said it was irresponsible to put these artworks in public spaces as people would deface them with graffiti. My response was that people had to get used to the idea of seeing art in everyday spaces and that they would not do anything to damage these works. That is exactly what happened. One of the works by Sanjiv Sinha was made of various weapons and it had the dove of peace perched on top of it. This was criticized as being violent since it had so many weapons on display. My response was that the symbol of peace was perched above those weapons. There is violence in every society and there are weapons too. What good comes of concealing this?

It was also decided to install artworks at the major intersections. To this end, a workshop was organized at a local art college. Various artists who were well-known at the national and international levels were invited to it. Pink marble slabs were imported from Jaipur. In fifteen days, these artists produced a variety of works. I had placed one or two local artists with each of the big artists so that they might watch them at work and learn from them. These artworks were then placed at prominent intersections on busy streets.

I had observed that in developed countries that whenever a cultural institute was set up, 1–2 per cent of the budget was spent on acquiring artworks for it. The first of these was the Karpuri Museum. A beautiful gate was made there and Mithila Banj artworks were installed. The CM's residence and office were also similarly enhanced. Eight senior artists of Bihar were selected and commissioned to prepare artworks that were put into the Gyan Bhavan entrance. The year 2018 marked the centenary of Gandhiji's Champaran Satyagraha in Bihar. Three famous painters—Jatin Das, Siddharth and Brahmdev Pandit—were commissioned to make a mural that had Mahatma Gandhi at the centre. This artwork, which was forty feet tall and twenty feet wide, was placed in the Gyan Bhavan and was admired by all those who saw it.

Statues were erected at all the spots Mahatma Gandhi had visited during his tour of Bihar. Azadi Park (Independence Park) was inaugurated on the occasion of the victory day of Bihar's brave son, Babu Veer Kunwar Singh. Murals depicting his life were put up in this Park. The four main spots he had visited during his fight with the British for Indian Independence were marked with victory pillars. Several laser shows were held to familiarize the people with Bihar's role in the fight for India's Independence; Guru Gobind Singh's life and the exploits of Veer Kunwar Singh. Such laser shows also take place on a daily basis at various places across Patna.

Bodh Gaya, which is a World Heritage Site, was developed and a new Maya Park was established there. Here, camps called 'Buddha Enlightened' were held for many years. Many artists from various countries came to these camps and made a variety of artworks. These were all put on display in the Maya Sarovar. International artists like Mona Khartoun were also represented.

Around 2,000 crores were spent on putting Bihar's art and culture on display. Besides the Patna Museum, other institutions such as the Samrat Ashok Convention Centre were also set up. An international convention centre was built in Rajgir with its own visual arts gallery. The Central Jail was right in front of Patna Junction. The prison was relocated and the Buddha Shanti Stupa was set up with a beautiful park and museum. A huge museum devoted to Lord Buddha is being set up in Vaishali. There is a plan to start an important Bapu Museum in Patna. A science museum designed to international standards will also come up in Patna. A convention complex of international standards is being built at Bodhgaya, which is an important tourist centre.

There is an old tradition of holding cultural programmes around the time of Durga Puja in Patna. Different pandals would be set up by local committees on their streets or at junctions. These programmes would run all night. The great and the good would come to perform there.

Patna audiences were renowned for their connoisseurship; I have heard many famous artists proudly say that they had often performed at the Patna Durga Pooja and that no artist considers themselves complete until they had performed at a Patna Durga Pooja in their lifetime.

But this tradition was dying too. The pandals would come up but the cultural programmes no longer took place. There seemed to be no money for the programmes, the organizers seemed to have lost interest and the residents were no longer actively involved. The State government decided that this tradition should be resuscitated and that the leadership of this effort should go to the department of Art, Culture and Youth. To begin with, there would be a two-day celebration which would bring together the most respected artists from across the country and after that, the pandal committees would take charge of organizing cultural programmes. The State government would provide economic support. With the help of a panel of experts in the field, we made a list of artists. The most renowned theatre directors, musicians and singers of the time were invited. We had classical music programmes and also ghazal and light music performances.

On the first night, the programme began at 7 p.m. Until 11 p.m., there was popular music and drama. At midnight, the classical music began. It seemed as if all of Patna had arrived at Gandhi Maidan. The programme lasted until morning and was enjoyed by all. The Chief Minister, several ministers and many prominent citizens were all present through the night. Many famous Biharis were invited, including Shatrughan Sinha, Manoj Bajpai, Prakash Jha, Shekhar Suman and Manoj Tiwari. On the second day, there was classical music followed by light music. We had invited the nationally acclaimed singer, Kishori Amonkar. She did not, however, like the number of the suite that was booked for her at Hotel Maurya and we had to change it quickly. When she came to sing at 10 p.m. in Gandhi Maidan, she began with *riyaaz* (practice). This did not go down well with the huge crowd gathered there. Another mistake was that the compere announced that after Kishori ji, Manoj Tiwari, the famous Bhojpuri singer, was to perform. The majority of the crowd could not understand the subtle nuances of Kishori Amonkar's renditions and so they began to shout, asking for Manoj Tiwari to come on.

I saw that the programme set up for the first night was the correct one. This idea of mixing the light and the classical was a bad idea. Kishori Amonkar left the stage in a rage and we had to run after her. It took the combined efforts of N.K. Singh, Prakash Jha, Manoj Bajpai, Shatrughan Sinha and Shekhar Suman to persuade her to agree to sing at 7 a.m. in a private gathering. Shri Krishna Memorial Hall, in front of Gandhi Maidan, was prepared for her and an exquisite two-hour programme of classical music followed. Here, thousands of people listened to her, deeply appreciative of her mastery. Others, including a tabla maestro and a classical dancer, observed that korma and kheer should not be served together. This was the idea with which I had organized the first day's programme: the popular music went on up to midnight and then we followed it with music for the cognoscenti. This Durga Puja Programme lasted through the two nights and no one wanted to leave. Another good thing was that all through these nights, no untoward incidents were reported, no thefts took place, nor were there were any reports of lost children. The next year, we offered economic support to some committees to do their own cultural programmes but this was met with limited success.

In 2005, when a new government took over, the decision was taken to make Foundation Day into Bihar Day but the question was which day should be chosen. Should it be the day on which Bihar was separated from the State of Bengal? Or was it to be the day on which the Governor took office in Bihar? After much debate, 22 March was chosen.

The idea behind Bihar Day was to reestablish pride in Bihar as a State. Hence, it had to be a festival, a celebration to remember. Bihar had a proud and long history. This was where Gautam Buddha and Guru Gobind Singh were born. Two ancient universities—Nalanda and Vikramshila—had flourished here. Patalipura, the ancient capital of Bihar, had been the capital of the country when it was even larger than it is today. This was where the great dispensers of justice and maintainers of law and order, Chandragupta Maurya and Ashoka, had ruled. This was the home of the mathematician Aryabhatt. The workers of Bihar had offered the sweat of their brow to set up far-flung lands such as Mauritius, Fiji, British Guiana and Surinam. And yet, its image had taken a terrible beating in recent times. To be called a 'Bihari' was an insult in cities like Mumbai or Delhi though these workers from the hinterland of Bihar were the mainstay, the backbone, of these very cities. Were they all to leave, these metropolises would collapse.

The first Bihar Day was celebrated in 2010 as the ninety-eighth year of the founding of the State. On the one hand, the progress the State had made was showcased and on the other, a host of cultural programmes relating to Bihar and India in general were also presented. There was also a food festival. Hundreds of thousands of people participated in the ninety-eighth and ninety-ninth editions.

Naturally, the centenary year had to be planned on a grand scale. It was determined that this time the celebration would drill down from the capital to districts, circles and villages as well; it would include colleges, schools and other institutions. The Bihari diaspora extends beyond India to many nations of the world. The plan was to involve many of them in the celebrations as well. Schools and colleges were spruced up. The children went out on *prabhat pheris* (dawn processions) and cultural programmes were organized.

A new logo was designed which became popular both across India and the world. The logos were made into stickers which people fixed on their scooters, motorcycles and cars. A State song and a State prayer were formulated too. People from across the State were invited to participate in the writing. Thousands of entries came in and a shortlist was prepared. The Chief Minister went through it. We approached Pandit Hariprasad Chaurasia and Pandit Shiv Kumar Sharma for the music to go with this prayer and song. Udit Narayan and Alka Yagnik sang the song. In the centenary year, the song became very popular across the State. It began to be played at various programmes across the State. The newly introduced prayer was taught in all schools. The hundredth year of Bihar was also celebrated by the diaspora in England, the US and Japan, among other countries.

Bihar lacked modern sports facilities. It was decided that Bihar Divas would be marked by the inauguration of a new sports complex. To make this event unforgettable, an international women's kabaddi tournament was held in which dozens of national teams competed. The Air Force put up a magnificent display of the Women's Paratroopers Wing. These brave women jumped from great heights out of helicopters, making splendid formations even as they unfurled the tricolour.

The entire State participated. There was involvement at every level and the public pitched in magnificently. Although the Education department led the initiative, it was the participation of the citizens that made it a memorable event. The preparations were so demanding that the intensive work we put in at the Education department caused some of us to fall ill. I had a minor heart attack. It all began with what seemed like a cough and a cold but I decided that this could wait until Bihar Divas was over. When I went to Delhi for treatment, the doctors were amazed that I had kept on working even though one of my blood vessels was almost completely blocked. A stent was put in thereafter.

Bihar received much attention for its work towards the empowerment of women. In order to encourage their participation in employment and social life, 50 per cent of seats at the panchayat level were reserved for them, the highest in the country. The immediate result of this was that half the seats at the district and panchayat levels were occupied by women. Positive discrimination was institutionalized in favour of women in all programmes of the government. Examples of this were the school uniforms and cycles schemes, which were first provided for girls and then extended to all.

When a girl child was born in a family, the family received a celebratory amount after she had an Aadhar card made and had been vaccinated. One-third of the jobs in the police and other government services were reserved for women. Fifty per cent of the teaching posts were also reserved for them. This brought about a change in the atmosphere of Bihar. Women began to appear more frequently in government and social programmes and their involvement in social empowerment programmes also increased. Institutions like Jeevika were set up to cater to the development of rural women; these centres were tasked with the economic development and health of Bihar's rural women. Women began to improve the lives of their families by creating and running self-employment schemes.

Once, I had the opportunity to visit a Jeevika Programme in the village of Sudur. A woman who had no schooling was the Treasurer and she explained the banking scheme to us—how they choose which scheme to support, how they calculated the interest, how the money was returned and how they kept accounts. We were amazed at her knowledge. We also heard that most banks were keen to support these Jeevika Programmes since their record of repayment was very good.

Slowly, the per capita income of rural Bihar began to improve. However, some of this increase in income began to be used for alcohol. Although the number of liquor shops did not increase, young men on motorcycles would buy country liquor in pouches and sell this in their villages and to their groups. Now, alcohol was coming to the drinkers; they did not have to undertake treks to the shop. A man who earned between three hundred to four hundred rupees a day could easily afford three or four pouches of hooch at twenty rupees a pouch. The production of country liquor increased exponentially.

This meant an increase in domestic violence. And since the liquor was cheap and accessible, children began to get addicted too. When I was surveying a development programme in the interior of Araria district, I discovered that children who were around fifteen or sixteen were loading bricks on tractors at brick kilns. Every two hours, the contractor would give each of them a glass of a liquid to drink. I thought it was a sharbat but later I discovered that he was giving them a glass of country liquor to speed up their work.

At many of his meetings, the Chief Minister would find a group of women waiting for him with an appeal to impose prohibition. This happened at the Srikrishna Memorial Hall where he was addressing a meeting of female self-help group workers. When he had finished his speech, some women in the audience began to raise slogans demanding the imposition of prohibition. He responded by saying that if he were re-elected, he would impose it.

And so the Chief Minister called for a meeting on prohibition. It was decided that prohibition would be imposed in a phased manner. In the first phase, the production and sale of country liquor would be stopped and in the district centres and other important places, shops selling Indian Made Foreign Liquor (IMFL) would be set up. The idea was that alcohol would no longer be available cheaply without country liquor and due to the reduction of the number of shops, access to alcohol would also become difficult.

When the first phase was successful, total prohibition was imposed. There were many articles in the media against the imposition of prohibition and questions were raised about its success. Some people maintained that prohibition had never been a success anywhere, in India or in the world. It was their contention that this was a matter of choice and people should be free to choose to drink or not. In developed nations, beverages with low alcohol content have become part of ordinary meals. Another contention was that prohibition would not end the sale of alcohol but simply force it underground. There was also the possibility that adulterated alcohol might enter the market with its own attendant dangers to the drinker's health and even survival. A third contention was that a poor State like Bihar could ill afford to lose the 5,000 crores generated by the sale of alcohol. It would also damage the tourism industry that was doing so well and the many hotels that were coming up.

Despite this, the State government decided to impose a strict programme of prohibition. As for the 5,000 crores, it was blood money. It was estimated that the 10,000 crores that families could save by not buying alcohol would be put to better use. That sum would be spent on children's education, health and furniture for homes, etc. These would also deliver taxes to the government. And it turned out to be true. In the first year, there was only a shortfall of 100 crores.

When the first stage of prohibition was announced and the plan of opening IMFL government-operated stores, the women strongly opposed it. The CM believed that if there was such widespread support for prohibition, we should move swiftly to total prohibition. Toddy tapping was also stopped and those who worked in that industry were given alternative work. Self-employment schemes were offered to the poor to prevent them from losing their income.

The government believed that prohibition would fail

unless it had mass support. The Education department led a huge campaign of mass education. The more than 1 crore students studying in the schools of Bihar got their parents or guardians to take the pledge. Government employees and officials also followed suit. The Vidhan Mandal gave it unanimous support. Song writers composed songs and sung them. Films were shot based on real-life events. The Literacy Campaign workers wrote millions of slogans all over the walls of the villages. Every district had art competitions. There were plays about prohibition. All this was aimed at creating the right atmosphere to bring in prohibition.

I also decided that to show solidarity in this matter, a human chain should be formed for thirty minutes. This was the first time such a large human chain had been organized in the State. There was no prior example of such a huge chain anywhere in the world and so massive preparations were made for it.

Four main roads running from north to south and two from east to west were chosen. Two crore people were expected to form this human chain that would run for twelve thousand kilometres. It was clear that we would need support at the local level to execute such a mammoth task. Many of the roads ran through areas that were largely unpopulated. People would have to be transported there. About 15 per cent of this trail cut through mountains or jungles or flood plains. This was a huge challenge: to move all these people to the required spot and then to get them back home again.

Although the human chain was supported by all political parties and organizations, for our own satisfaction, we decided to document this event via the Indian Space Research Organisation (ISRO) through its satellites. The ISRO team arrived but they informed us that the satellite surveillance from national and international satellites would last only up to 10:30 a.m. Our human chain was to be formed at 11:30 a.m. They also told us that the satellite could just cover a twenty-kilometre-wide stretch and only that would be recorded. Nor would the people forming the chain be visible. They would only appear like a mist.

Considering these problems, large signs denouncing the use of intoxicating liquors and supporting prohibition were prepared and displayed at the main cities of the State: Patna, Muzaffarpur, Darbhanga and Gaya, among others. These appeared clearly in the satellite images. We knew that some people might ask who the participants in the human chain were and so lists were made at the village and local levels and these were published. Photographs were taken and helicopters were deployed to gather footage of the human chain and a film was made on this event. A pamphlet titled 'Na Bhooto, Na Bhavishyati' (Never Before, Never Again) was published by the Department of Education. The *Limca Book of Records* also recorded this as the longest human chain. The beautiful aspect of this was that most other human chains had been formed against something done by a government. This was the first human chain to be formed in support of a government initiative.

Some intellectuals went to court to protest the involvement of children in this human chain. It was our contention that we had not used young children and that the older children who participated would learn an important life lesson. Social change is as vital a lesson as any. Since this was a government initiative, we had organized ambulances, drinking water and first-aid medicines. We wanted to make sure there would be as few accidents as possible during this human chain event. Several accidents take place in Bihar usually, but the pleasant surprise was that only three accidents happened that day.

Women and children participated to a heartening extent in this human chain. Under the leadership of women, the majority of the families took part in the human chain and so in many areas, the line was two- to three-people deep. In order to make the whole thing successful, the women had put in place many other interesting elements including mehendi, rangoli and songfests. Although the inspiration was the Chief Minister's and the direction was in the hands of the government officials, it seemed as if the people had really taken ownership of the human chain. Bihar was in the throes of a festival and every family was a part of it.

Bihar is one of the most populous states of the nation. We have the highest number of people per square kilometre. The cities of Bihar are ancient and they have, like Topsy, 'just growed' with no underlying plan. This means that there is a shortage of open spaces in most urban areas. The State government wanted to improve this situation and so it decided to build a number of parks and plant trees by the side of the roads. There was also an attempt to develop public parks in as many areas as possible so senior citizens in the area could step out for some fresh air, children could find a place to play and adults could take a morning or evening walk.

A huge, filthy nala (channel for water) flowed past the Patna Secretariat, carrying waste and effluents. It filled the place with a foul smell. The idea was to make this entire area into a park. Huge pipes would carry the waste water to a treatment centre and then the project of transformation would begin. The area was divided into three to aid further development.

There were few spaces in Patna for children to play or for the youth to do exercise. So a large space was developed as a park for them. Exercise machines young people would need were put in. Jogging and walking paths criss-crossed the entire park. Two water bodies were set up at which boating and other water sports could be enjoyed. Various spaces were created for music performances.

One part of the park was the Ashok Vana—full of the favoured tree of the Jain Tirthankara. Small groves were designed on the basis of astrological signs and Sikh symbols were also incorporated into the design of these groves. A profusion of flowers and trees, including palms and cycads were planted so that the biological diversity of the world might be introduced to the citizenry. The third area was given over to adventure sports. The whole place was named Rajdhani Vatika. Eminent sculptors from across India were invited to create a sculpture park in which a work by the world-famous sculptor Subodh Gupta is also featured. Other prominent artists like Rajat Ghosh and Sanjiv Sinha are also represented here. These public sculptures have become 'selfie-points' for tourists and passersby and are part of the public's visual memory now.

There were few places for morning walks in Patna so it was decided that the area between the Secretariat and Raj Bhavan would be developed as a recreational space. A variety of plants and trees were planted to showcase Bihar's biological diversity and a moram track was developed. A herb garden of medicinal plants was set up near the Chief Minister's quarters. This was also thrown open to school children so that they might enjoy it and see different species of plants in one place. Now there are dozens of parks in Patna where thousands of people enjoy fresh air and children are free to play. This was replicated in other districts as well.

Since I had worked for a long time in the Education and Health departments, I had a long association with the courts. When I was in the Health department, doctors had filed so many cases that I made it a practice to visit the High Court for updates on the cases before going to my office. At one point, things came to such a pass that I asked the Solicitor General whether I could have a small space assigned to me in the courts so I could get my work done properly. Most of the cases were about the terms of employment, wages, etc. Some of these people had not worked at their places of employment for years but were demanding benefits and promotions. A few had taken appointments aboard and having returned, wanted to re-enter the Bihar Medical Service.

Some of the cases reached the Supreme Court, making my attendance there necessary. I had to be personally present or risk contempt proceedings. Since I had so many dealings with the courts, I began to understand its systems of administration and protocols: what to wear, what posture to adopt, how to reply to questions.

The case I refer to here took place at the time when I was the Chief Secretary of Bihar. It was the height of summer. I was wearing black trousers, a full-sleeved, light-coloured shirt and black leather shoes when I went to court. And yet, the judge took exception to my clothes. Neither I nor the government lawyer accompanying me could understand what my sartorial faux pas was. The judge, however, was appalled. He said that he would not hear the case until I came appropriately dressed. He even went on to ask me how I would feel if the officers under me appeared before me dressed as I was. I realized how far removed he was from ground realities. Most of our officers wear ordinary clothes; no one wears a suit or a bandhgala to work.

I was surprised that in 2018, the court could expect a government officer to appear in a suit or a bandhgala and that too, in that weather. But the judge was adamant. He would not hear the matter until I presented myself suitably attired. I asked for the hearing to be shifted to the next day and went straight to Connaught Place. I had four thousand rupees with me. In the shops, I found that a readymade bandhgala costs six to seven thousand rupees.

One of my friends took me to Chandni Chowk where I bought a bandhgala for three thousand two hundred rupees, and dressed in it, presented myself at the Supreme Court. And so, my contempt was purged. When I returned to Patna, I gave the bandhgala to a dear friend. I had no desire to keep it.

I prefer workers over thinkers. I did not like the kind of officers who gave impressive presentations but could not get their hands dirty with the actual work. I preferred the ones who spoke little but worked a great deal, and praised them highly.

The United Nations was out in full force in Bihar. I would joke that without stints in Africa and Bihar, the lives of a UN official would not be successful. They were forced to come to Bihar because we were high on the poverty index. These institutions had their own agendas which often did not coincide with what the State needed. They had their own programmes of social change. My belief was simple: we needed economic and technical assistance but in the areas that we determined. Also, we did not want visitors; we needed organizations that would work with us and stay with us. And slowly, we began to see the change in them and we got the help we needed. Some organizations such as DFID, the Bill and Melinda Gates Foundation and Pratham did good work in Bihar. Teams from these organizations lived in the State and worked with the associated officials.

7

Memory Bank

There was one big thing I could not achieve during my long term in the Bihar IAS. Some attempts were made but they did not succeed. Bihar had a convention by which it was more important to appear honest than to actually be honest. If someone were to earn money by his hard work, he would not get the kind of respect he would earn in other, developed places. It is assumed that good earnings have bad roots. If someone has become rich and successful it can only be because he has used foul means—I understood this very early in my tenure.

In those days, I was the District Officer of Vaishali and the Managing Director of the Industrial Development Authority. As part of my remit in the latter role, I was responsible for bringing in good industries to the area. They were to be provided with facilities and their problems had to be resolved. But whenever I met with an industrialist, I made it a practice to have another official from the Administrative Service there. It raised doubts if one met with an industrialist alone. I had the same problem when I was working with the Bihar Industries department. Once, a prominent industrialist wanted to invest in Bihar and meet with the Chief Secretary. He invited him to lunch at the Maurya Hotel to talk things over. I was surprised when the Chief Secretary refused the offer. He told me that having lunch with an industrialist in a five-star hotel would generate unnecessary suspicion. It was rather startling to me to think that even a five-hundred-rupee lunch was seen as enough reason to cast aspersions on someone's honesty or to make the assumption that he/she was being influenced.

I asked the Chief Secretary how it came to be that his office had neither a waiting room nor a toilet. I was aware that in many States, the Chief Secretary of Industry would not just meet with the representatives of industry but also receive them at the airport. Their entire focus was to impress the industrialists with ease of business and to offer them such facilities as it would bring investments into the State.

At that time, there were many States that were doing their best to attract investments. This led to benefits not just for the State but also for the government. Bihar, however, led the States in the way it mistreated representatives of industry. These were seen as people on the make. The business sanvedak (contractor) had the reputation of wanting to make a lot of money for themselves and were also poor on delivery. It was supposed to be a hugely profitable business, and therefore, it was very difficult for any sanvedak or supplier to get any money out of the government. There were hundreds of ways in which money that was due could be left unpaid or at least, the payment dramatically slowed down. And at each level, someone had to be paid off to get a sum that was due. One of the officials high up in the hierarchy made an attempt to improve the dignity of the sanvedak and the supplier. A joint training was organized. Their complaints were heard and a scheme to reward good work was put in place.

When I joined the Department of Education, someone in the Basic Infrastructure Authority got together with the Managing Director and worked out a new scheme of payment. In this scheme, a representative had to go to the location of the work, shoot photographs on his/her mobile and load these updates on the computer. These were examined and the money would be deposited in the account. No one had to keep coming to the department to collect dues. Even when I was in the Department of Education, I had dealings with sanvedaks and suppliers whose payments I made on the spot for events like Bihar Day and the National Youth Festival. When for instance, huge tents had to be put up in Gandhi Maidan, the appointed suppliers would receive 20 per cent of their payment in advance. This put some heart into them and they worked with a will and delivered work on time. In a similar fashion, I paid artists 50 per cent of their fees at the time of signing. The other half was handed over just before they went on stage.

When it was decided to pay Subodh Gupta one crore rupees, I made an advance payment of 50 lakhs. My colleagues in the department pointed out that if the artist were to die before delivering, recovery would mean legal proceedings. The other point they raised was that it was only after the goods/services were found adequate upon inspection that payment could be made. I explained that these should be changed and there should be some trust between the government and its contractors and suppliers.

This was the way we worked with the Bihar Museum project and it was totally justified. I kept monthly tabs on the work. Generally, the government Inspector would find fault with the work and let the contractors have it. But my major concern was with the work and the payments. The contractors and suppliers had begun to trust us and it was important for the department to ensure that payments were made before the meetings. If the department did not release the allotment or the engineers did not give their approvals, things could get very bad. Many of the artworks meant for the Bihar Museum were being constructed abroad. The officials would review the work and make the payment based on how much of the work had been completed. And so, the job was done well and delivered on time. But it was not possible to bring about a holistic change in the change in the way payments were made since the bureaucracy was set in its ways and those ways had hardened over time.

In the last few years, one of the greatest problems that has plagued our land is the way everyone seems to be trying to do other people's jobs. This had led to friction between the major institutions—be it the Lok Sabha, Rajya Sabha, State governments, the judiciary, the executive and the media. The respect they have for each other has eroded. And they all play one-upmanship games with each other. Certain institutions which are supposed to be independent and have no political affiliation such as the Auditor-General, the CBI, the IB and the Enforcement Directorate are losing the faith of the common man as political interference increases.

Now each department has two or three bosses. The courts demand a huge amount of officials' time via personal appearances. The committees of the State government exert unwarranted pressure on them. There are hundreds of high-level review meetings. Most officials find it difficult to get on with their work, to make plans and initiate projects since they spend most of their time fire-fighting.

Very few bureaucrats act with initiative and energy. A large chunk believes in making no decisions at all; their contention is that these decisions might end in an inquiry. They become experts in finding legal reasons for their inaction or when they find one, at inventing imaginary ones. Very often, suggestions or projects are sent off to the other departments such as the Law department or the Finance department for opinions merely to delay them. This is a class of so-called honest officials who take home salaries of 2 to 2.5 lakhs but do not work. In every project, they only spot flaws.

And often there is a clash between the politician and the bureaucrat. This is mostly because the politician knows he/she has been selected for a period of five years and wants to do as much as possible within that time. But for the bureaucrat, the timespan is one of twenty to thirty years and so he/she sees no reason to hurry. India must be one of the last countries where one can get a permanent job up to the age of sixty. Those who choose to take up this work, try to avoid any work.

There are also those who see their salaries as pittances and are always on the lookout for ways in which to augment their income. The 'extra' is called 'speed money'. When officials get something done, they believe they have done the person a favour and do not accept the fact that it is their responsibility to do that job.

8

The World Before Me

An International Youth Festival was to be held in Cuba. India was to send a contingent too. I was the in-charge Director of the Arts, Culture and Youth department. Abdul Bari Siddiqui was my Minister. We created a team of nine folk artists. It was decided that the team would be led by the Minister and myself, but the proposal was rejected at the Centre.

At that time, very few officials or government contingents went abroad. One of the officials of the Finance department asked me what could possibly be the benefit of participating in all this. It was our contention that this was one way to bring Bihar's folk art and traditions to the world's attention. I also pointed out that our only expenditure was the air tickets; all the rest would be taken care of by the Cuban government. But when we were still denied, I told the Minister to talk to the then Chief Minister. The Chief Minister had just taken over. He told the Minister to write down on a piece of paper what had to be inscribed on the file. I wrote that the journey had been approved and that the required formalities would be completed on return. And we got ready to go abroad.

Since there were only two days left for the event, one of the tickets was booked from Delhi. The total cost of the tickets was Rs 7,50,000. The money had been released. It was placed in a suitcase and since there were no high-denominations notes, it filled up the entire suitcase.

The money travelled as my hand luggage to Delhi. As the case went through the scanner at the airport, I was stopped and asked what I thought I was doing. I replied that I was a government servant on my way to Delhi to buy air tickets. Though they were rather surprised, I was allowed on board and the tickets were booked after we reached Delhi.

When I went to the embassy for our visas, the Cuban Ambassador was listening to Hindi songs on the radio. This gave me a boost. He looked at our forms and raised his eyebrows since the inauguration of the Youth Festival was the next day. I told him that if he gave us the visas, he could leave the rest to us; we would make it there. He laughed and said that truly God must be in charge of running the country, but he gave us the visas.

Cuba is an island nation a hundred or so miles to the south of the USA. It is a country of sugarcane fields, also known as the land of Fidel Castro. When we arrived, we were told that each member of our group had been placed with a different family. The Minister and I were assigned neighbouring families. Cuba is a beautiful country whose climate is also salubrious. Each day would dawn bright and clear but slowly, the temperatures would rise and by about noon, it would rain. Daily, I set out in the morning in crisp clothes which would be drenched in sweat by noon, making me want to bathe again. The family I lived with would hang my sweaty clothes out of the window. They would dry and be ready for use again. There was no smell. I was surprised to find that there were no bad smells in the toilets or of sweat. Later, I discovered that their food was cooked without spices which might account for the lack of odour. That didn't stop me from bathing twice a day though.

The government had supplied the family with provisions to last us the week of the festival: bread, rice, vegetables, meat, fish, eggs, tea, coffee, milk, mineral water bottles and rum. I kept the bread and eggs and left the rest for my host family. Since the cuisine had no spices then, it was all boiled, bland food which palled quickly. I found a vegetable that resembled capsicum which offered the vague suggestion of a chilli. Eventually, bread and eggs with the ersatz capsicum became our staple. We had brought some crunchies and sweets with us as gifts but the Cubans found the savoury snacks far too pungent for their tastes. They would taste them and immediately eat something sweet to cool their mouths down.

Cuba was poor but it had good health and education systems. The government took it upon itself to ensure that every citizen had access to education and health care. Salaries were equitable there was hardly a 10 to 15 per cent difference between the salaries of a bus driver and a professor. The good thing was that everyone had a ration card on which they could get everything they needed for the month, this included food and also soap, wine and rum. It was up to the family in question whether it used the soap in a week or eked it out for a month.

There were separate shops and restaurants for tourists. Residents had no access to these. Telephoning was inexpensive. In the neighbourhood in which I was staying, the government had presented someone with a car. This prize of a car was awarded annually, I was told, to the person who had done the most work. That year, it had gone to a driver in the army. They did have television but there were only two boring government channels.

I found that the older generation had a great love for the country and were ready to make any number of sacrifices for it. This was not the case with the younger generation. They resented the tourists who came to Cuba, flashing their dollars and enjoying themselves. But then, the young Cubans were the ones who bore the brunt of the housing crisis. Building a house was something of an enterprise in Cuba. Buildings of five to six storeys were erected. Each family that wanted to live there had to contribute a day's labour. President Fidel Castro had also taken part in this. But there were still long waiting lists. Young couples were often forced to live with their parents after marriage and neither the parents nor the married couples seemed happy about this.

Che Guevara was still a force to reckon with. His memory was kept alive and the majority of the young people sported T-shirts that had a picture of his face. Boxing, volley-ball and football were popular sports. Each neighbourhood had public facilities for these.

When we were totally fed up with the bland boiled food, we went to a five-star hotel on the pretext of drinking coffee. We did drink the coffee but we also commandeered the sachets of pepper from every table. These we used to spice up the food. Black coffee and bread were widely available. That could be had in every restaurant. Everyone drank their coffee black. Milk was for children and convalescents. Most of the buses in Cuba were a gift of Soviet Russia. Sometimes, two buses would be joined together and driven.

People wore the minimum required clothes. Most of the children roamed around in shorts. And music rippled out of everywhere, rhythmic, lively. Groups of young people needed only a guitar and a riff to start singing.

Our guide was a school teacher who knew a little English. I asked her to organize a visit to the Botanical Gardens. Cuba is famous for its biodiversity and is especially renowned for numerous endemic palm species. I was deeply impressed by the Botanical Gardens and wanted to take with me as many seeds as I could. When I talked to the Director of the gardens and she discovered the extent of my knowledge of and curiosity about succulents, she agreed to let me have some seeds. She made only two conditions—I should name all the succulents in the garden and I should only carry as many seeds as would fit in my pockets.

The next morning, I got to the gardens in a tracksuit which was equipped with plenty of pockets. I asked the guide to wear my other tracksuit. Together we managed to collect about 400 seeds. The Director made an inventory of these so that the Customs would not stop me. Cuba has strict laws about taking seeds out of the country. I brought home 400 seeds of twenty species from Cuba.

One day, I had returned to the house in which I was staying after taking part in a programme. After bathing, I was shovelling down lunch when someone came running from next door. The Minister was ill, he said, could I come? I hurried over and found the Minister lying down. I asked him what was wrong and he said he was quite all right. Turns out that no one takes a siesta in Cuba so when they saw the Minister lying down, they got frightened and thought he was ill as only someone who was unwell would lie down in the middle of the day.

Even the way people got jobs in Cuba seemed extraordinary. First, one had to accumulate points by doing social service. My guide, for instance, started off as a waiter, working three days a week in a restaurant. After some months, she was taken on as a regular waiter and could work every day. Then she began taking orders for the restaurant. And finally, she got a job as a primary school teacher.

The head of the family in which I had been placed was a retired Police Chief but twice or thrice a week, he did traffic duty. When there were important visitors, he was often on security detail. It seemed to be the policy that one should work for as long as one is able to.

At the airport, when we said farewell to our guide, I wanted to make her a gift of twenty dollars but I only had a fifty-dollar note and a hundred-dollar note. As we were going on to France, I needed the hundred dollars to spend there. So I gave her the fifty-dollar note. The teacher was very happy but she would not be able to spend the money so I used it and bought her soap and some creams. I also gave her the tracksuit.

When I was on deputation to the Central government in the Human Resources Development department, I got the opportunity to do an MBA in Australia sponsored by the Commonwealth. I was admitted under this scheme to the Southern Cross University. The Australian government gave me a family scholarship. In 1999, therefore, I went to Australia with my family. I had two young children both of whom were in the early years of their schooling. The main campus of the university was in Lismore, New South Wales, a beautiful and vibrant city. There is a Hindi film song which goes, *'Phoolon ke sheher mein ho ghar apna'* (May our home be set in a city of flowers) and this felt true of Lismore. It had blue skies and an unpolluted environment. The population was low and the civic amenities outstanding. You entered a bathroom and were greeted by the scent of flowers.

I got an opportunity to live at both campuses over the course of a year. There was a great contrast between them. The first six months were a wonderful time from our point of view. There were mountains and forests that offered ample opportunities for trekking. The next six months were at the Gold Coast Campus which had just been constructed. The area was also being developed for coastal tourism and there were many tourists from Japan and Singapore who were out for a good time. Two floors of a multi-storey building were set aside for us. There was also an e-library.

The family scholarship from the Australian government covered the bare necessities but not the comforts. The rent took up more than half of it. The children's school fees were paid for and every three months, there was a hundred-dollar scholarship too. I took 1 lakh rupees with me of which I used sixty thousand to buy a second-hand Toyota to make travelling to the university easy and so that we might see some of the country as well. Most of the students with us couldn't wait to sell their cars once the course was over. I didn't do that because I wanted to make the best use of my time and to that end, I would need a car.

Our children, being very small, slept with us. But it was the Australian way that each child should have their own room so we had to hire a three-bed room apartment. The floors were made of wood or were carpeted to keep the noise of our footfalls from disturbing the neighbours. One could only mow the lawn on a Sunday morning. The dealer who had got us this flat had video-graphed the place and showed it to us and had also made an agreement that we would have to return the flat in the way that we found it or lose the two-thousand-dollar guarantee, which would be claimed as damages. This meant that we had to be very careful to make sure we left the fittings undamaged.

When I went to Australia for my MBA, I was around forty years old. I thought the students would all be much younger than those of us who had come on the Commonwealth Exchange Programme. But I found that about half of the class was my age. Things are different Down Under. The students complete their school education while living at home with their parents. Only some of the students go on to get a higher education. Most take up vocational courses and find a job.

As they earn, they learn. In other words, they pay for their own higher education. And so, the four-semester MBA course which we were going to complete at a stretch, they might finish in parts. Higher education in Australia is expensive and cannot be completed without parental help. The other surprise was the complete absence of household help. For instance, only the very rich could afford a driver. However, ready-made meals were freely available; one had only to pop them in the microwave and they were ready to eat. Yet, my wife spent much of her time cooking meals for us. All of us did our share of the cleaning. Our family was basically non-vegetarian, with a preference for fish. In Australia, people ate their fish filleted, cutting out what we thought of as the good bits. The heads and tails—the aforementioned best parts—were sliced off and thrown away. Chicken feet and necks were also disposed of in this manner; again, these were the parts we relished.

Once, I went to a wholesale market which sold entire fish. When I asked the seller to slice it for me, he said that it would cost me almost as much as I had paid for the fish. Because of this, we bought a good knife and began bringing home whole fish and cutting them up. We bought chicken feet at low prices from the places where they were slaughtered.

In general, we found that the average Australian had great respect for India. India was seen as the land of non-violence, truth and the birthplace of several major religions. Many people knew who Mahatma Gandhi was. A number of Punjabi boys had married Australian women. Indian men were seen as good providers who did not think about divorce. The majority of these Punjabis were into farming and horticulture and using chemical fertilizers, they had tried to increase yields, but these began to poison the ground water and soil. When we would visit the weekly markets, we would see Australian women at the stalls while a Sardar ji was waiting in the truck.

The population of Australia is very low; a continent settled by one-third of the population of Bihar. When we spoke of lakhs and crores of people, we would be met with incomprehension or else though to be speaking in hyperbole. Since we spoke English, navigating Australia was easy. But we had classmates from China, Japan, Singapore, Malaysia, Italy and other European nations who faced a language barrier. Nor did they have as much experience as us.

Our Australian professors were always surprised by our lateral thinking and our out-of-the-box solutions. At one point, we had to write a paper on the Cola wars. We had to suggest ways in which Pepsi could grab some of Coca Cola's market share. Most students suggested the usual restructuring of management, cutting prices and improving packaging. I offered this idea: Coke bottles were to be tampered with; foreign substances introduced. The resulting bad publicity would reduce their market share. This solution startled them.

The teachers in school also admired our children's ability to count without calculators. At that time, no child could multiply or divide without electronic assistance. When I said that every Bihari could do this in their heads, they were astonished at how advanced we were in mental mathematics.

When I went to Australia, I could not use a computer because they were not in common use. But university-level work was all done on the computer. No professor would accept handwritten submissions. And so, necessity proved to be the mother of education as well and I learned how to use a computer. However, my typing speed was rather slow. A fifteen- to twenty-page research paper would take me three or four days and that too if someone dictated and I typed. This display of weakness delighted my son. He offered me a deal: he would type for a dollar a page. For the first two semesters I was forced to accept this but slowly, I learned to type. And I began to use email too.

For two semesters, we were at the Lismore campus. The next two were at the Gold Coast campus. The Gold Coast is an incredibly beautiful tourist area. It had all the facilities that a tourist might want. Huge numbers of tourists came from Japan and Singapore. Our university occupied two floors of a multi-storey building. The rest were given over to cinema halls, markets and other commercial enterprises. I had never seen a university like it. There were huge lecture halls and a computer room with more than a hundred units. The professors arrived fifteen minutes early for their lectures and stayed for fifteen minutes afterwards. Questions could also be emailed to the teachers. The campus had only an e-library, accessed through computers. We slowly acclimatized. I was placed first when the results were declared; the second place went to another Indian student from the Railways.

I had chosen this university with the idea of pursuing my interest in horticulture. There were jungles close by and many collectors of rare plants. I made a survey of all the major nurseries in the area and collected a number of rare plants. My wife shared this interest. We had gone on several treks into the jungles. We often got lost. You could walk for hours without meeting another human being or encountering a human settlement.

Another problem was that when I drove, my hand had a tendency to reach for the horn, whereas Australian drivers rarely use the horn. It will only be used if an accident has happened or in an emergency. It took a great effort of will to keep my hand off the horn. Parking was a major problem; spaces would have time slots. If you overstayed your welcome, you would get a photo of your car and an order demanding a fine. The entire traffic ran on a system of cameras.

At the time of admission, we opened bank accounts. It was a huge branch but there were only two workers. We were also allowed two free visits to the bank a year. Any more and we would have to pay a service fee. Most of the work could be accomplished via phone banking. You could pay for utilities and rent over the phone. That was where I first used an Automated Teller Machine or ATM.

Gold Coast was much more expensive than Lismore perhaps because it was a tourist town.

Mauritius, it is said, is an India far away from India. One feels right at home there. Mauritius has a deep and old relationship with Bihar. Between 1840 and 1880, thousands of Biharis went to Mauritius as labourers in the sugarcane fields of the British. About half of Mauritius' population has Bihari origins and Bhojpuri is an important language. People of Bihari origin have become Prime Minister, President and Members of Parliament. Mauritius and India have always had cordial diplomatic relations. India has contributed a great deal to the building of the island's infrastructure. We wanted to deepen ties and invite some of the Bihari Mauritians to come to Bihar for a tour. We hoped that as they went back to visit the places from which their ancestors had left India, they might see opportunities to invest in Bihar's development.

The Chief Minister was invited to visit Mauritius; I was included in his party. We were given a warm welcome in this island of the Indian Ocean. High-end tourism is well-developed there. Its beaches are white sand and water sports are well-maintained.

During our four-day stay, we visited temples and other religious institutions. There is a Ganga Lake in the mouth of a dead volcano; the then Prime Minister Shivsagar Ram Gulam had brought some Gangajal from India and poured it into this lake and named it Ganga Lake. We had brought along Gangajal from Patna and fish made of silver. These were ceremoniously offered to the Ganga Lake by the Honourable Chief Minister.

Bihar's impress is clear on Mauritius' food and clothes. The older generation still speaks Bhojpuri. Dal ki puri is a celebrated dish. The spot where the immigrants first landed is called Aapravasi Ghat (Immigrants Ghat) and has been tagged by UNESCO as a World Heritage Site.

We went with a cultural troupe that performed folk songs of Bihar at various places. We were welcomed by the Mauritius government with a programme that included a re-enactment of Bihar's contribution to the development of Mauritius. The early immigrants lived lives of toil and struggle. They laid the railway lines, built the roads and prepared the land for cultivation. All this has been captured in the folk song and folk theatre traditions of Mauritius. When we visited, the Prime Minister was Navin Ramgulam and the President was Aniruddh Jagannath, both with Bihari roots. Navin Ramgulam gave the Honourable CM a personal walking tour of his constituency, an unforgettable experience. The roads were lined with people raining flowers down on these dignitaries.

Each immigrant's details were summarized in a register in Mauritius. People could use this to find out which caste they were, where they had come from and when. We suggested that this be computerized. We offered assistance to anyone who wanted to return to their roots, help in locating their village and even, if possible, their relatives. I enjoyed my time in Mauritius, we were never far from the sea and there was an amazing variety of seafood. Mauritius has a flourishing tourist industry. Indians have also invested heavily there.

To strengthen ties between Bihar and Mauritius, the Honourable Chief Minister decided to install a life-size statue of Shivsagar Ramgulam, the founder of modern Mauritius, in Gandhi Maidan. Two years later, the statue was unveiled. The Prime Minister of Mauritius, Ramgulam Naveen was invited to do the honours. He is the son of Shivsagar Ramgulam. We organized a grand welcome and took him to see the village from which his ancestors had come. A huge cultural programme was held in his honour at

Gandhi Maidan. He was much impressed by a performance of the Bihar Gaurav Geet. He asked if this programme could be repeated in Mauritius and we sent the team to Mauritius.

Bihar Chief Minister Nitish Kumar was very keen to see Pakistan. He specially wanted to visit Takshila for a better understanding of the Indus Valley civilization. When the Pakistan government extended an invitation, the Chief Minister put together a team which included me.

Pakistan does not issue a national visa; instead, you get a city visa. India returns the favour. And so, we got visas for Islamabad, Lahore and Karachi. We got a visa to see Takshila after we arrived in Pakistan.

When we got to Islamabad, we were given a royal welcome. It was Deepavali time. We were invited to dinner with President Asif Ali Zardari on the night of Deepavali. The Chief Minister received a beautiful carpet as a gift. At Rawalpindi, we went to cricketer-turned-politician Imran Khan's home at his invitation. He expressed his admiration for the Bihari formula for progress. He had invited all the leaders of his party. They had a long discussion with the Chief Minister on the policies and programmes that had been implemented. Islamabad is a modern city, built to a design specified by modern city planners. From Islamabad we went to Karachi.

The influence of the army was clear in Pakistan. Officers of the Pakistani Army accompanied us from the time we arrived at the airport. They seemed to be present on every street and at every intersection. In ordinary conversation, too, the people spoke of the army carrying out functions usually allocated to the police. This was even more apparent in Karachi. The law-and-order situation here was worse than in other cities and the citizenry seemed subdued.

Karachi has many residents who have Bihari roots. We were told that Karachi has the biggest population of Biharis, nearly 20 lakhs, outside Bihar. Some had gone to Karachi directly after the partition. When Bangladesh had been established, some had moved to Karachi. We were given a very warm welcome. We went to visit the bazaars and bought some clothes. The shopkeepers showed great respect and gave us huge discounts. I found that Pakistan resembles north India a great deal. The styles of eating, dressing, even the body types and faces seemed very familiar. There was no language problem either. Everybody spoke Hindi fluently. Their major demand was a simplification of the visa process so that they might visit their relatives in India. They had a great liking for Indian goods too. But these came via Dubai and other countries and so were very expensive. They wanted unrestricted movement and commerce between the two countries. The armies were often at loggerheads, but the people believed that good neighbourly relations could be established. The Governor of Karachi invited us over to dinner. When we arrived, the Governor said that his wife had given instructions that we should be treated well, as guests from her home town. She was abroad at the time. Her ancestors had emigrated from Sabzibagh, Patna.

After Karachi, we went to visit the ruins of Taxila, or Takshashila. It is regarded as one of the earliest universities of the world, perhaps a bit older even than Nalanda, the great ancient university which flourished in Bihar between the fifth century BCE and the twelfth century CE.

At its peak, Nalanda had as many as 10,000 students and 2,000 teachers. Science, astronomy, medicine and philosophy were taught at this university using Hindu and Buddhist streams of thought. It was one of the great centres of Mahayana Buddhism. At Vikramshila, Vajrayana Buddhism was taught and tantric subjects were part of the curriculum. There were two other great knowledge centres at the time: Telhara and Udantapuri. The excavations at Telhara have led to the belief that this was also a Mahayana Buddhism site and that nearly a thousand bhikshus lived here. Telhara is now regarded as a contemporary of Nalanda; it is believed that after completing a course of study at Nalanda, the monks would go to Telhara for higher studies.

Unlike Nalanda, the entire site of Takshashila has not yet been excavated. The ruins, however, tell us much about the settlements of those times. The site was on an elevation near a river. It was clear from the ruins that the civilization had an advanced system of waste disposal with bathrooms and drainage. Homes were built according to a formula. The excavation of Takshashila had been started by the British before Independence. We went to the site museum too. Many images of Lord Buddha in the Gandhara style were on display. There was a beautiful display of all that had been excavated from vessels to ornaments to implements of daily use.

Our last stop was Lahore, the capital of Pakistan's Punjab province. We met Nawaz Sharif there who was no longer the Prime Minister. He had a house with hundreds of acres of land around it. The house itself was a palace with every modern convenience. There were animals and large birds—among them, peacocks, cranes and ostriches—roaming freely, on the one hand, and there was a helipad on the other. Nawaz Sharif did not lack for confidence. He was sure that he would become Prime Minister in the next election and indeed, he did win the election.

The Chief Minister of Pakistan's Punjab province at the time was Shahbaz Sharif, Nawaz Sharif's younger brother. He held a dinner in our honour. We met the leading citizens of Lahore. We also visited a village with one of his ministers to see what village life was like. It seemed very much like the village life of Punjab. The British had built a good irrigation system here using canals. There were huge orchards of fruit trees. Agriculture was well- developed.

Touring Pakistan felt like we were touring another Indian state. The division between the rich and the poor, however, seemed wider and deeper. There were some very rich people who had acres and acres of land. The land ceiling was fixed at five hundred acres per family. The rest of the population was terribly poor and eked out its living. The top hundred Pakistani families sent their children abroad to study. They dominated the country's politics, business, justice system and army. Although there was a local police force, the impact of the army was clear and omnipresent. There were terrorist attacks in Karachi often. Everyone walked in fear of the army and few ventured out on the streets after sundown. As an Islamic country, there was prohibition, but alcohol was available for tourists in five-star hotels. There was a fine tradition in Pakistan by which one could serve only one major dish at a wedding. Wasteful expenditure was not the norm.

We got the opportunity to meet with Hindu and Sikh minorities. Some seats were reserved for minorities in Parliament. We also visited Hindu temples and Sikh gurudwaras. We went to Nankana Sahib where the head wanted to touch the Chief Minister's feet as well as ours since we had come from Patna Sahib and so were sanctified and this gesture would elevate him spiritually.

Later, there was a meeting with officials of Pakistan's polio eradication campaign. Pakistan still had a problem with polio. We had run a polio eradication campaign successfully in Bihar and the Chief Minister explained our battle plan. All the office-bearers in Bihar had been enlisted in the struggle and tasked with the responsibility of making their respective areas free of polio. They were told that they could deploy government servants of any department to go and administer the oral vaccination. The Chief Minister's office kept an eye on the campaign. The message for the authorities in Pakistan was this: the debilitating disease could be eradicated if it were made a national priority and the participation of the general public in the campaign was ensured.

The Asian Games were held in Hangzhou between 12 and 27 November 2010. I went there with the Indian kabaddi team. We were the unchallenged gold medallists and expected to win gold again. In the finals, the Indian men's team defeated the Iranian team and the women's team defeated Thailand. Kabaddi was developed in India and then it spread to other countries. I was associated with the Kabaddi Sangh for a long time. We would send coaches to various Asian countries to train them. Slowly, other teams began to get better. Iran, South Korea and Thailand were all getting good at the game. When the men's and women's teams won gold, our national anthem was played. This was a moment of pride.

It was my first trip to China. The biggest problem was language. Ordering breakfast was a hurdle. Only a few people at the hotel reception spoke English. Lunch orders had to be conveyed via Google Translate. Finally, I found a translator thanks to the Indian Tourist department. I learned a lot from him, including the fact that one had the right to personal property up to the age of seventy because that was considered the average human life span. It was difficult to transfer personal property as well. The government decided who would live in which city and where their children would study.

Hangzhou had also updated and modernized to hold the Asian Games. I was told that the city had built more than a hundred flyovers in three years which sounded unbelievable but it was true that there did indeed seem to be many flyovers. People in the city took their time over food and drank tea rather than water. The first time I had a meal in China, a kettle of hot water was placed in front of me. Green tea leaves were put in it and I drank the tea in small cups. At first, this wasn't very appetizing but eventually, I grew used to it and green tea became quite a favourite. Soya was ubiquitous. I ate loads of vegetables, fish and eggs. Hangzhou has a saying, 'If it moves, it can be eaten', presumably with exceptions made for planes, trains and automobiles. Chinese food in China was very different from Indian Chinese. Most of the food was boiled and did not feature any spices. I also found out that they enjoyed eating things as they are found in nature. So if you ordered fish, you got the whole fish with head and eyes and tail and fins.

I discovered another interesting food habit when we went to a restaurant once. There was a hot plate in the middle of the table and on it, a pot of boiling water. Whatever one ordered was brought to the table and one put it into the water and cooked it. One put in what would take time to cook quickly and kept adding other things later. For example, I would put in chicken first, followed by fish, then vegetables and finally, any leafy green vegetables. One ate in the opposite order. First the leaves, then the vegetables, followed by the fish and finally, the chicken. There were condiments—salt, chillies, soya sauce—which one added if one wanted.

Once, when I was returning from the stadium to my hotel with a tourist guide from the Chinese Tourism Department, I saw some women waiting for a taxi. I got out of my taxi hastily, carrying only what was in my hands. The women got into the taxi and it pulled away. It was only then I realized that I had left both my mobile phones in the car. My guide tried to retrieve the phones but in vain. The taxi driver was contacted but he said that the women who had hired the taxi had made an abrupt exit about two kilometres away from the hotel. Perhaps they had taken the phones with them. Now I was stuck in a foreign country with no telephone numbers and no way to contact anyone. Nor was it easy to get a new connection in China. I could only remember my landline number in Patna. Finally, my guide got a phone in his name and I called Patna and retrieved some important numbers. I managed with this for the next four or five days.

Hangzhou had been done up for the Asian Games. It sits on the banks of the huge Qiantang River. A night trip on the river was a wonderful experience. After a few days, it became clear that China's cities were well-developed but the countryside was still plagued by poverty. It also became clear that the laws only applied to the common people. These who were associated with the party were exempt. It was difficult to change the government's policy decisions. For instance, if the government chose to widen a road, the land would immediately be vacated by those who lived there. This could not be dreamt of in India.

I visited China a second time for the Bihar Museum. The contract for the fabrication of the interiors had been awarded to a Singapore-based company—City Neon, one of the best in the business. City Neon had its fabrication done in the south-eastern city of Xiamen, China in the Fujian province. Most Singapore-based companies do their fabrication in China or Malaysia. They say that they do not want to increase pollution in their country nor do they want to put too much stress on the nation's infrastructure.

Xiamen is a small, beautiful city. A lot has been invested in building roads. A little distance from the highway stood rows of huge trees. These were planted in advance before the roads had been planned because tree-lined roads were preferred. When we visited the rural areas, we saw two campuses of two hundred acres. I asked whether this was to be a university and was told it was empty for the time being. What was to come up there had not yet been decided. I found that quite surprising. The other thing I discovered was how impossible it was to get the Chinese to talk about their government. Their faces always had a smile on them and they thought before speaking.

We went to a Buddhist temple in Jiamin. The gate was decorated with a huge Laughing Buddha; inside, there was the standard version. Buddhism is popular in China and Lord Buddha is revered in much the same way as Lord Ganesha is in India.

☙

I visited Singapore since City Neon had been awarded the fabrication contract for the interior of the Bihar Museum. Although Singapore is a tiny country, it is very well-developed and a technological marvel. It is difficult for a person to have more than one car there. Even those who have cars can only drive them on alternate days. So everyone uses public transport. Cleanliness is a priority; littering attracts a fine of a hundred dollars. There were no false ceilings in the City Neon offices. The utility ducts and pipes were not hidden; the company works as a team so even the Managing Director's cabin exactly the same as that of his colleagues'.

We visited the major libraries of China and Singapore. I

did not see any security in the form of police officers. There were no traffic policemen to guide the traffic either. The people were very disciplined. Although there was a great deal of racial diversity, they lived together amicably. Government housing and schools were well-developed. Getting a flat or admission to a school was based on membership in a community. Children from all communities studied in the same school, building feelings of fraternity and friendship.

There was a new educational experiment in Colombia called Escuela Nueva. I was sent there by UNICEF to study this model. The problems in the field of education that Colombia had resembled the problems India faced. They too had a shortage of teachers and resources. We had to visit schools in and around Bogota and Cartagena. We stayed at a hotel in Bogota, the capital. I had another reason to be excited about visiting Colombia. Cycas Zamia grows there, but in the mountains, which have been colonized by the drug cartels. I made friends with a young man and struck a deal with him: I would teach him yoga and he would drive me around Colombia in his car. I would also pay for petrol and food. He warned me that Cycas hunting would not be easy so we should look for them in the nurseries and botanical gardens of Bogota. The Botanical Gardens of Bogota were large and beautiful but they did not have the specimens I was after. They had not succeeded in collecting them from the mountains. It was very difficult for ordinary people to travel there.

So I changed my plan and decided to study Colombia's rural life. We went to a village about a hundred kilometres from Bogota. The people there eat corn as a staple. Different kinds of bread are made from corn and it is also distilled. I was eating lunch in one part of the village; the food was bland in the extreme. I asked the bearer whether people did not eat chillies there. He came back with a chilli on a saucer with two toffees. I saw the point after I tried the chilli; one really did need the toffee.

There was a festival on in the village. Everyone was wearing colourful costumes and making their way to a small stadium nearby where a bull-fight was to take place. This was my first viewing of a bull-fight—a play between the sport and dance. I saw two museums in Colombia. One was a gold museum in which all the display objects were artworks made of pure gold. A great deal of gold was to be found in Colombia. There were many ancient *objets d'art* made of gold; I had never seen a museum of gold before. Colombia is also known for its emeralds.

The other museum had different types of corn seeds. In the past, more than thirty different types and colours of corn were grown. Slowly, these strains began to die out in the name of productivity. Now only two varieties dominate the landscape. This is a good example of how man thoughtlessly destroys biodiversity.

Colombia had recently undergone an educational revolution. The investment in education was comparatively low. Short on teachers, they also did not have enough room in their schools. The Escuela Nueva model had some new ideas to address the problems. If there were two rooms in a school, then the students from the first to the fifth standards would be divided up by their level of ability and seated in groups. The furniture was also modular and could be reorganized at will. All the equipment, maps and books were placed in one corner of the room. A child who needed an instrument or a book could take it from there, use it and then return it. There was not enough to give each child his/her own books. The children were not allowed to take the text books home unless they had been ill.

Dividing children according to their level of ability meant that the teacher did not have to spend too much time with the bright ones. These advanced students often acted as teachers. They would also sit with the students from junior levels and solve their problems and read to them. In this way, two teachers could handle a school of a hundred children. The emphasis was on practical experience rather than bookish knowledge. So if the lesson was on a common illness, the homework assignment would be to find out more about it from their family and neighbours. They might discover preventive methods or cures from these sources. Hence, they would learn a lot that was beyond the curriculum.

The Colombians were astonished to hear that we give every student all the books of each and every course. Why would we need to waste so much paper? And why weigh down our students with all that paper? Their textbooks lasted for years since the books never left the school.

Their teaching style was also different. In India, we have a separate directorate for teacher training. There are courses specifically created to train teachers and they undergo specific training programmes. Colombia's method of training was innovative. If there were thirty schools in an area, all the teachers would gather in one of the schools on a holiday, once a month. They would talk about the problems they had encountered and share experiences; if another teacher had experienced the same problem, he/she could share the solution they had found. This was how they used their experiences to innovate. I admired these small experiments in education that were being conducted in Colombia. No huge expenditures were being made. There was no giant bureaucracy at work there.

Italy is a world leader in the field of art and culture. Every city is a repository of great art and music. The Italians count Leonardo da Vinci, Michelangelo, Sandro Botticelli and Caravaggio, artists who are seen as Old Masters, among their ranks. Among the musicians there were Giovanni Pierluigi da Palestrina, Monteverdi, Domenico Scarlatti and Niccolo Paganini. Opera began its life in the seventeenth century in Italy. I started my Italian journey in Rome, which is the capital of the modern State of Italy, but it has also been the capital of the Roman Empire. The Colosseum, a world-renowned monument, is situated here. Rome also cradles Vatican City, an independent State. The Vatican has its own museum which is outstanding. It also has the Sistine Chapel whose ceiling was painted by Michelangelo. The Vatican Museum is full of the works of famous painters and sculptors. There are hundreds of pieces in the sculpture gallery. It seems as if there isn't enough room for all the treasures. And of course, it is thronged by thousands of tourists. The crowds make it difficult to take in the artworks at leisure.

But it was Florence that left a deep impression on me. It is one of the hallowed birthplaces of the Renaissance. The art, culture and architecture are unparalleled. The Duomo and the Basilica di Santa Croce define the skyline. Michelangelo's David stands there in the Academia Gallery. The Uffizi Palace has an unrivalled collection of art. Giorgio Vasari was the architect of this palace, home to the Medicis, in which hangs the works of Leonardo da Vinci, Rafael, Caravaggio, Titian and Giotto.

Florence has an important place in world history. Many seminal art movements, including the Renaissance, the Baroque and Mannerism began here. It has a history of being a rich city, its wealth based on business. The residents will tell you proudly of the time that the King of England was in debt to Florence. The quarries around Florence have beautiful marble which may explain why it produced so many noted sculptors.

The third city I visited was Milan. This is considered the commercial capital of the country. Its fashion industry is world famous. Football is hugely popular. Leonardo da Vinci's famous fresco, *The Last Supper,* can be viewed by appointment at the Santa Maria delle Grazie. The country's largest cathedral, Piazza del Duomo, built in the Gothic style, is also here. There is a Museum of Ancient Art which is well worth visiting. I had been to many countries and their museums but the art in Italy surpassed them all. In matters of art, Italy is, in my opinion, the foremost in the world.

Italy is also the land of pizzas and pasta. There are many regional variations. The wine is renowned too. I went to a small restaurant more than a hundred years old on advice from my hotel. This was old-fashioned pizza—bread with cheese and tomato. They serve it with a rosé. This was very different from all the pizzas I had ever eaten. In India, we load the pizza with a great many toppings, making it much heavier.

Japan is my favourite foreign country. I went there many times. The first visit was when I was Secretary of the Tourism Department. Several teams from India had gone to Tokyo to promote tourism. Our job was to get tour operators interested in what India had to offer so they might spread the word among their clients. The embassies of both nations supported this endeavour. However, we had to pay for all expenses incurred whether it was hiring a space or organizing a press conference. I was at the end of my tether when I found myself thirsty at a conference venue. I was told that I could buy some water from the vending machine. When I explained that I was a speaker at the conference, I was told that I would get a bottle of water when I went on stage to speak, and only when I did was I given a 100 ml bottle of water.

Bihar holds a special place in the minds of those who follow Buddhism. This is where Lord Buddha achieved enlightenment. He spent much of his life in various places in Bihar. Bodh Gaya is to the Buddhist what Mecca-Medina is to the Muslim. Every Buddhist hopes to visit Bodh Gaya at least once. And yet, there were not many Japanese tourists there. I wanted to know what we could do to change this. Most tourists from Japan come on chartered planes, carrying their own food and bringing an English-speaking guide. These are not high-value tourists for they spend very little money in the State. I told the tour operators that we were in the process of developing Vaishali and Rajgir, both of which were important Buddhist sites. Thus, they should expand their itineraries and create two- to three-day excursions. At that time, we were also considering building a golf course because the Japanese are very fond of golf.

We had long conversations with the tour operators. They told us that we would have to pay greater attention to cleanliness at Bodh Gaya and Gaya. Most tourists go there for spiritual reasons so there would be no real advantage to a golfing green. They also emphasized the need to improve the roads. They pointed out that while food was inexpensive in India, the hotels were far too expensive. The kind of hotels we had on offer in India were available at half the price in countries like Thailand. Other tour operators suggested that there might be scope for medical tourism in Bihar as medical procedures were costly in Japan.

After the conference, there was lunch which we paid for, going Dutch. When we were eating, a woman said that we should continue our conversation about developing tourism in India. This was the first time I was simultaneously eating my lunch and speaking into a mike, which was placed on the table in front of us.

There were over 600 rooms in the hotel at which we

were staying. Language was a problem. This was where I saw a Japanese garden for the first time. A small area in the hotel had been beautifully landscaped, with a stream in which colourful fish swam. There was a wooden bridge to cross it. There were only a few plants in the garden and they were bonsais.

It was all geometry—white pebbles and huge boulders in conversation. I would sit on one of the rocks and contemplate the garden and a great feeling of peace would descend on me.

The Tourism Minister accompanied me on this trip; he wanted to see the important cities of Japan. I had a friend who ran a restaurant in Tokyo and I asked him to take the Minister on a Japan tour. A rail pass was bought for the Minister. The bullet trains of Japan are famous and this made it possible to consider going to all the important Japanese cities within the next three days.

Japan has one of the finest collections of rare plants. Although the majority of succulents originate in Africa, Mexico, USA and Latin America, the Japanese have developed a marked expertise in growing them and developing hybrids. I often went to Japan to learn some of these techniques.

Masato Yokai and Yashomichi Hiroshe have co-authored and self-published a three-volume work on variegated plants. These plants are rare. If they occur, they are invaluable and collectable. This book has become very popular since it has pictures from all the great collections in the world. When they were working on the fourth volume, the authors went to Thailand. They wanted to see all the important collections of South Asia. Someone in Thailand suggested that they come and see my collection in India. When they visited Patna, they were deeply impressed. They found thirty to forty new variegated species and took pictures of them. I also gifted them many plants. A few days after this meeting, Masato Yokai passed away. When I visited Japan for the first time on a plant-collecting expedition, Hiroshe-san kept me company for five days and took me to see all the most important collections in Japan.

The Japanese tend to be secretive. They do not want just anyone and everyone to see their collections. When they have developed a new varietal, they share it among themselves in Japan first. Only after a few years have passed do they allow the outside world in on the new plant. But since I was with Yashomichi Hiroshe, I faced no such problems. He is a well-respected figure in Japan. Every collector or nursery threw open its doors to us and I had quite a fine collection of samples afterwards. Some I bought and others were gifts. The Japanese know how to respect rare plants so they do not use tissue culture to mass produce specimens. They only use natural means to grow them, either through cuttings or seeds.

This is the exact opposite of what happens in China where they use tissue culture to propagate new specimens in huge numbers to sell them cheap. These generally tend to be weak and unhealthy.

I bought a rafis variegated plant in Japan. The seller gave me a booklet with the plant, which had the entire story of the plant: its antecedents, how it was propagated and monthly photographs. It was a four-year-old and there were fifty photos of it in the book. Their documentation is brilliant. Every job is done with great attention.

There are auctions for these plants in Japan. I attended one and watched as a plant sold for 5 or 6 lakh rupees. The Japanese are good at showing their respect for a beautiful and rare plant. They use the best methods. Their nurseries, like those in Thailand, South Africa and the US, are never very large. They raise their plants in small spaces with the most modern techniques. The emphasis is on quality rather than quantity. In some nurseries, one must disinfect one's feet before going in to prevent the entry any viruses or bacteria into the collection.

I wanted to see the succulent nurseries of Japan and

meet the important collectors. An expert who had become a friend agreed to take me around. We would leave early in the morning and return only at night.

When I ran out of funds, I borrowed some from the Minister. The Japanese are punctual and not given to wasting words. It is difficult to get them to talk but once they become friendly, things get easier. On this trip, I made many gustatory experiments. Sushi became one of my favourite snacks. Raw fish is often used; the fish is so fresh it can be eaten raw. I also ate octopus and other exotic seafood. Japanese food is not just nourishing and fresh but it is also served in artistic styles. In a Japanese meal, there should be elements of earth, sea and sky. They believe that the food will be better if many colours are represented on the plate. The Japanese are renowned for their discipline and their unity. They bring their all to their work.

My second visit to Japan was for the Bihar Museum. The architects of the Museum were Japanese. We were to see some of the buildings they had designed. It had been decided that cotton steel would be used to build the Museum. This had been used to make some buildings in Japan. We wanted to know what affect the rains and wet weather would have on the buildings. We looked at some of Maki's buildings in Tokyo and went to a few libraries where cotton steel had been used. Japanese architecture is minimalist; there is not a single useless element in their design. Their designs use natural light and air.

I found their work new and exciting. We saw many museums in Tokyo and visited the Shimane Museum of Ancient Izumo by Maki. Cotton steel had been used on the outside walls. Maki's team was with us. The road to Shimane wound past Mount Fuji whose upper slopes were buried in snow—a lovely sight. The mountain was beautifully lit. Maki invited us to dinner and gave us a presentation of all his major works and their special features. When we returned to India and received the bill, our share of that dinner was marked to us. Most people go Dutch in Japan.

My third visit to Japan was as a member of a team accompanying the Chief Minister who had been invited by the country. During the course of this visit, we met with the Prime Minister, the Defence Minister and other high-ranking officials of the government. The Indian embassy in Tokyo had a seminar on the potential for investment in Bihar. We made our presentation on investment possibilities and outlined our experiences with Maki and the Bihar Museum. That had a great impact on the Japanese.

We then went to Kyoto and saw the Hiroshima Memorial. The bombing of Hiroshima in World War II caused immense loss of life and property. Some of the bombed buildings have been preserved. A museum also shows the various aftereffects of the bomb and the extent of the damage caused. Some of the images in the museum moved us deeply. There was an imaginatively organized display of the half-burnt items of daily use such as cooking utensils, a bicycle, clothes and the like.

After Hiroshima, we went to Nara, the capital of Japan between 710 and 794 CE. The tallest image of Lord Buddha is to be found in a temple here. It is fifteen metres tall and weighs 500 tonnes. This remarkable temple is made of wood. It is known as Todai-ji. The Nara Park is close by. A herd of deer lives in the Park and is used to the attention of tourists.

Nara has an important connection with Bihar. They explained that the bhikshu who started the ceremony of opening the eyes of the Buddha had come from Bihar. Some of the stones that were used to pave the road to the temple had been brought from India. Along with Lord Buddha, there were images of other historical persons too. This wooden temple has suffered damage at the hands of many attackers. There are wooden models of what earlier versions of the temple looked like.

The Governor of Nara invited us to lunch. We were served lunch in bento boxes. This is a beautifully organized packed lunch which includes many small items. It is famous in Japan. Each region has its own variants of what is served in these dark wooden boxes. Each bento box therefore is a buffet of local culinary delicacies. We discussed the friendship between Bihar and Nara with the Governor who seemed enthused.

There are a number of Indian businesses in Japan. The Consul General hosted a dinner for us in Kyoto to meet Indian businessmen there. There are Indian restaurants to be found in all the important cities of Japan. Some of them are very popular. And so, we often ate Indian food on our journey. Japan is an expensive country. Its hotels and bullet trains cost a lot more than such services in India. It is also the best country to see new inventions but the Japanese way of life seemed dreary and mechanical. It's not the kind of place a Bihari like me could settle in.

New varietals are to be found in the largest numbers in Thailand for it has thousands of nurseries and collectors. I wanted to study these in detail so I took ten days accumulated earned leave and went to Thailand. In those ten days, I visited all the major nurseries of the country and met many seasoned collectors.

Each day, I would leave the hotel at 7 a.m. after breakfast only to return at 10 or 11 p.m. Not only did I get hold of many new plants but I also learned new ways of propagating them. The Thai people were soft-spoken and helpful. I made many contacts that matured into mutually beneficial relationships. Thailand has such good weather that one can grow plants right through the year. The temperature varies between 20°C to 30°C through the year—the best range of temperature within which to grow plants. There is no shortage of water either; there is adequate rain. In the world of horticulture, Bangkok is the Calcutta of Thailand; Calcutta's temperatures also allow for such cultivation.

Thailand's nurseries import plants from across the world, especially Japan, and then propagate them in large numbers. They are also cheaper than in Japan. It is not difficult to bring new plants into Thailand because the Customs officials understand the economic importance of the plant business. The only rule is that there must be no soil on the roots, through which diseases may enter the country. It is easy to get a quarantine certificate from Customs.

When I brought home my selection from Thailand, mine became one of the world's great collections. Then I began to gather rare plants from across the world. And slowly, I built a reputation in this world of plants. This meant that many people would also be willing to exchange plants with me. When a collector from another nation visited, he/she would bring plants for me. Some stayed with me and this deepened our friendship. I would also direct them to the best nurseries and the serious collectors. Now this was a passion with me, an addiction one might say. A day that I did not spend some time with my plants seemed a day that was incomplete.

I went to Ethiopia on behalf of the London Growth Centre. The International Growth Centre of the Department of International Development (DFID) has its headquarters at the London School of Economics. This organization is tasked with assisting backward nations with a variety of schemes to help policy makers research and create policies. From the beginning, the International Growth Centre has had a centre—the Asian Development Research Institute (ADRI), in Patna as well. Many of the schemes in Bihar have been studied under its aegis by international experts.

I was to participate in the annual meeting of the centre, to which all the countries in which it was working in were invited. I had to describe the story of Bihar's progress. Ethiopia is in the north-east of Africa. Like India, it is a tropical country. Its capital is Addis Ababa. It is one of the oldest civilizations of the world. It also hosts the main office of the Centre for African Unity or the African Union. There are offices of every African country here. Like many other African countries, it is a developing nation. It is famous for its coffee and its long-distance runners. There are more than a hundred languages here and most of the people are Christian, Muslim or Jewish. Eighty per cent of the population lives in the countryside. Injira, a kind of leavened bread which is eaten with meat or vegetables, is the staple food. Coffee is very popular and it is generally drunk without milk.

After my speech, I went to the museums and art galleries. The National Museum was in bad shape. However, the culture deeply impressed me. Most of the artefacts were made of wood. There were only a few metal objects. I saw a number of masks that the original residents wore. These were strongly influenced by the natural surroundings. The masks of different clans were different and so were the masks used for various occasions. I could distinctly see the roots of Cubism as it developed in Europe. Their modern and contemporary art bore clear indications of their struggles and of their close connection with nature. China has invested a lot in Ethiopia's progress. Many bypasses and overbridges were being built by Chinese companies. It was clear that they were looking at a long-term association with Ethiopia. One night at dinner, I met the famous runner Haile Gebrselassie. He was about five feet five inches tall and a friendly person who did not have any airs even though he was an Olympic medallist. He was now coaching the Ethiopia team.

Most of the succulent plants in the world come from South Africa or Madagascar so I travelled to both these countries.

Madagascar's biodiversity is truly astonishing. The long island has a wet northern section while its southern half is dry. Most of the succulents are to be found in the southern half. Madagascar is a developing nation with a law-and-order problem. I had contacted the Worldwide Fund (WWF) before going there. They were my hosts in Madagascar. Although it is rich in natural resources, the country is poor. It had been colonized by Britain and France. At the Antananarivo Airport, the immigration officer asked for a hundred dollars. I had been told this would happen and was advised to say that I did not have dollars with me. The officer was smart; he said he would take Indian rupees. I gave him a hundred rupees.

The WWF had sent a car for me. The door of the car would not close so I spent the entire trip holding it in place. But the driver was a friendly soul. The driver spoke English which was a godsend. He told me about the economic privations and the law-and-order problem. I expressed my desire to see the plants in the jungle in their natural state. I was staying at a three-star French hotel but would be using it only as a place to sleep. I bought some essential ingredients and the driver agreed to get them cooked at home and bring me food.

I purchased bread, eggs, vegetables and fruit and gave them to the driver. I had two bottles of rum with me and I handed over one of these to him. He was delighted. I was in Madagascar for four days. Every day, the driver brought me a breakfast of bread and eggs and a packed lunch. If we felt hungry, we ate whatever was available along the way.

There was a high level of unemployment in Madagascar.

From time to time, our car would be stopped by unemployed youth who would ask for money. The driver told me that I should keep some notes in hand. He would negotiate with them and decide whether I should pay or not.

We needed help from the locals to find the plants I was looking for. To see some, we had to trek to the mountains. It was a completely new experience for me to see the small specimens or seeds I had bought growing large and wild in their natural settings. The older generation told me that thousands of the best specimens had been uprooted and taken to the West. The WWF was now assisting the government in an attempt to protect those plants. The WWF official took me to meet Mr Alfred, an expert in succulents. He had discovered many new varieties of euphorbia and palms some of which carried his name. His collection was large but the plants were not in good shape. And he was over seventy-five years old and a drinker too. Before showing me his collection, he insisted I take him to a nearby bar and buy him a drink. We did so and he came back in a cheerful mood. On my day of departure, he gave me the plant specimens he had promised at half the rate he had originally quoted.

Now came the problem of documenting these plants. He packed them in cartons and called a Customs official. We went back to the bar and then the Customs official checked them in for me. I was able to bring a big and beautiful collection of rare plants back to India from Madagascar.

※

In South Africa, I made Johannesburg my centre of operations. The Consul-General was a Bihari. He knew that I was coming in search of rare plants but he had no idea how obsessive I was. Other than a dinner with the Ambassador and a museum visit, I spent most of my time on looking at good collections, meeting with collectors and chasing after plant specimens. Johannesburg has the Apartheid Museum which tells the story of race in that county. Mahatma Gandhi is deeply respected and there is a life-size statue of him in the city centre.

South Africa is a very modern country in terms of infrastructure, often resembling a European nation. There are many mines that once yielded gold and diamonds. It is now a free and democratic country but there is still a great deal of work to be done to bring about equality between the Blacks and the Whites. There were once areas that were 'White Only' and Black townships, marked off by barbed wire fences.

In fact, I was told that it was in South Africa that barbed wire was first used to control human movement. The physical resources of the country were still largely under the control of the White-skinned residents. They had amassed a lot of land for themselves and so many of the plants that should be in the jungle were now to be found on personal property.

Since I was the Consul-General's guest, I was vouchsafed opportunities to see these plants and learn about them. We were crossing a dry jungle to get to one of the famous nurseries. This was in the foothills of a huge mountain. It was around 4 p.m. when we got there. It took us about an hour to go around the nursery and make a selection. The owner said it would not be possible to pack the specimens and give them to us for it was already 5 p.m. and the workers left sharp at five. The owner told us that he was required to sound a hooter at 5 p.m. to indicate to the staff that they were free to leave even if some work was left incomplete. This made it clear that the workers who were Black were aware of the rules and their rights but also that they did not have much interest in their work. We placed the specimens in the car ourselves and took them back to the hotel.

I had to leave the next day. In our excitement, we had taken some large specimens. They would not fit into my suitcase. I emptied the other suitcase which had my books and clothes. I left these with the Consul-General and filling my suitcases with plants, set out for home. The Consul-General was astonished to see my passion and he began to take an interest in plants as well.

France has been the capital of the world for its art, culture and literature. For decades, artists, musicians and writers have been going to Paris to make a name for themselves. Paris is also a city of museums. The Louvre, held to be the greatest of the world's museums, is there.

I had been to Paris before but then I was in search of rare plants. Nor was I so interested in museums. But when I went to Paris for the Bihar Museum, I stayed in a hotel which had been a haven for the city's art community in the dark times. They would dine at this hotel and share their sorrows. They would pay their bills in paintings. There were only a dozen or so rooms in the hotel, each named after a famous artist. When I asked to be booked into this hotel, the embassy was surprised. They said it was listed as a three-star hotel but hardly merited it. I was adamant because I had heard that each of the rooms had an artwork by a great artist.

The hotel turned out to be in a downbeat area, in a small gully. As I had travelled to many countries, I had arrived in France with two big suitcases. One of them was filled with plants and artefacts. When I reached my hotel room and opened the door, I had to spend a considerable amount of time figuring out where those suitcases would go. The toilet was also tiny. I would need to use the room to meet friends and artists. I wondered what I would do if three or four people were to visit me at once and indeed there was an occasion when I did have three visitors. One of them sat on the bed, one on the chair and the third opened the door of the toilet and sat on a stool inside it.

The embassy was right, it did not seem like a three-star hotel. Even by the standards of Paris—where apartments can be tiny—my room was unusually small and cramped. But to balance all that, there was a beautiful painting hanging on the wall behind the bed.

Small rooms would appear to be the norm in much of Europe. Once, I went to Delft, a Dutch city, to do a course in the management of water resources. The toilet in my hotel room there was so tiny I had to bend almost double to enter it. There was barely three feet of clear space around the bed. A small table stood at the edge of the room with a chair tucked into it. I came to believe that it was the intense cold that accounted for this; larger rooms would need more fuel to heat.

Lord Cultural Resources, our consultants, had helped set up the programme for Paris. I was assigned a docent who was an expert in museology and art. We were to begin our tour of the museums the next day. I could not invite the expert to my room and so, in true Indian fashion, I invited him to join me at breakfast. He accepted but said he was already on the clock. His daily fee was a thousand euros. So we had a hasty breakfast and left for the Louvre. The Director of the museum welcomed us. We spent the next four or five hours immersed in a study of the great artworks there. It was as if all the best and the most beautiful objects of the world had been brought together in the museum. I had to see the *Mona Lisa* of course but it left me cold; there were other works by da Vinci which seemed far superior. When I asked why it was so significant, he said that it was possibly the first portrait done to a correct scale.

I saw hundreds of white marble sculptures which seemed almost otherworldly in their beauty and grace. On our way out, I thanked the Director for his time. He asked how I had liked the museum and I said that though there were many beautiful works, they were not displayed well. Perhaps this was because the original building had been a royal palace, constructed for royal comfort and royal tastes, rather than as a modern museum. Beautiful sculptures were placed on floors that clashed with them. The sculptures stood where the royal children had practised their riding. Modern lighting was also impossible in a heritage structure.

The Director seemed rather piqued by my critique. He had probably pegged me down as a bureaucrat with no vision of what a museum should be like.

After the Louvre, we went to the Pompidou Centre, which is considered one of the greatest collections of modern and contemporary art in the world. It was extremely modern in comparison to the Louvre. It had been established as a modern art centre in the first place.

There was an open space in front of the centre where artists could present their work. Many were presenting their art at that moment. It has a welcoming air as if it is inviting you right in. Huge, colourful pipes make their way around the building. These pipes supply the building with water and electricity and other civic necessities. Even the staircases are not inside the building but have been built along the sides. I wanted to know which artists were represented in their collection. I was told that they had works by Subodh Gupta and Anish Kapoor. I was surprised to learn that none of the other contemporary artists about whom one hears so much in India were not featured here.

I liked the halls where the exhibitions were held. When I visited, there was a Salvador Dali exhibit on. Along with the Dali paintings, there were works by his contemporaries as well as information about the music and the fashion of their time. In a year, the centre does two or three exhibitions, each running for about three months. A great amount of research goes into every exhibition. The curators determine everything from the movement of visitors to the colour of the walls and after the exhibitions are over, the galleries return to normal.

The Director of this establishment invited me to dinner in the restaurant on the roof of the centre. It was supposed to be sea food but when the food arrived, it consisted of three or four kinds of fish served on a bed of crushed ice. There was a salad, baguettes and cream cheese to go with it. I thought the fish would be steamed or boiled at the very least but I found that they were really, truly and thoroughly raw. Somehow, I managed to get a few raw prawns down and then ate the salad and the bread and cheese. Eating dinner at 6 p.m. was also a new experience. I was told that people generally finish their dinner by 7 p.m. but the Director was an extremely well-informed woman and I learned a lot from her. The next day, we went to the Musee d'Orsay which was once a railway station. They have a superb collection with many beautiful paintings by Van Gogh, Monet, Renoir, et al.

There are two ways to see all of Paris at one shot. One is to get to the top of the Eiffel Tower and the other is to climb to the top of the Montmartre hill to see one of the world's most beautiful cities spread out in front of them. Montemartre is part of the story of many famous painters who, in their time of struggle, lived here because it was cheap. In terms of geographic spread, it is much smaller than New York or London but it is far more beautiful. It has a plethora of ancient buildings which house museums. The people here are very refined and like doing things in style. They are proud of their language and culture. When I went to Paris for the first time, I asked a police officer where I could get a taxi. He told me the word for 'taxi' in French and would not answer the question until I had used the appropriate French word. The French revere their culture and heritage. They see the British as a nation of shopkeepers.

I went to London three times. The first time was to receive the Skoll Foundation Award. The Skoll Foundation was established in 1999 and awards a peace prize in developing nations. This award is also given for bringing about a positive social change. That year, three people were chosen to receive the award and I was one of them. I was rather surprised and wondered how I came to be selected. I found out that it was for the work in the field of education in Bihar. An NGO called Pratham also worked with us. Madhav Chauhan had founded this organization. Chauhan and I were both chosen for the award. When I asked why, I learned that the award was given because 2 crore children had been given school uniforms, cycles, scholarships and textbooks and if one put all this money together, it was one of the greatest investments made anywhere in the world in the cause of the education of children. It was then that it came to our attention that it was quite a formidable sum even in dollars. The title of the Skoll Foundation's report on our work was: 'When the Elephant is Shaken'. In their metaphor, the government was the elephant which is always difficult to move and with whom a new initiative is tough to achieve. I had to explain how we had shaken the 'elephant' at the programme in London. I heard that people from different countries had to pay a fee of 200 pounds to participate in the programme.

This would be the first time that I was speaking to representatives of nations from all over the world. I told Madhav Chauhan that it did not seem right for me to praise the government of which I was a part and therefore, perhaps it would be best if he were to present and I fielded the questions. We were given two hours to present and it became clear that our audience was astonished that a poor State like Bihar could have thought to invest so much in education. Some of the questions that came up after the presentation were asked by representatives of multinational corporations. A few of them wanted to design a software for the programme and others suggested that they could develop a model for the monitoring of such a huge investment. It amazed me that people could be thinking so quickly of how to monetize even this programme.

Our hotel in London was once a jail. Very little of its external appearance had been changed but inside, it had all the modern conveniences of any hotel. I had a friend in London, a doctor, who wanted to come and pick me up at the airport. I told him that it would be better for him to come straight to the hotel and to bring dinner—rice and meat—with him. When I reached the hotel, I set down my luggage and went to wash up. When I stepped into the bathroom, the floor felt warm to my feet. This gave me a start. I was afraid that there was some electrical problem and rang the reception. They informed me that since the floors are very cold over there, they warm them. However, if I wanted, I could lower the temperature myself. That was the first time I had experienced warmed stone floors.

I cleared up the room and lay down on the bed to wait for my doctor friend. Jetlag claimed me and I fell into a deep sleep. When my friend arrived, he asked the reception to buzz my room but they refused to wake me up. He was forced to leave the food at the reception and I ate it the next day and apologized to him for the inconvenience.

My second trip was on the invitation of the International Growth Centre who wanted me to tell the story of Bihar's success. This time, the Bihari doctors of London invited us to dinner. The International Growth Centre is located in a crowded area of the city. I thought there would be about fifteen or twenty Bihari doctors but there were fifty present with their families. I had taken forty Mithila paintings with me but I fell short. It was really an enjoyable experience talking with them. Many of them had very successful careers in London.

My third visit to London happened because of the Bihar Museum. I visited the main museums of the city and met influential people of the art world. The most important museum in London is the British Museum. It bears comparison to the Louvre in size and diversity of collections. At one point in its history, the sun did not set on the British Empire and this gave them the opportunity to collect artefacts from cultures around the world and display them in a beautiful manner. There is a separate collection of Indian artefacts and artworks which leaves one with mixed feelings.

At one level, one regretted the loss of these beautiful objects which have been taken away from the country but one also felt proud at the beautiful display and the obvious care that was lavished in their maintenance. Here, people from around the world can see and appreciate the magnificence of India's achievements in art and culture. I said jokingly to the Museum Director that it was perhaps time to return these objects to India since we now had good museums in which they would be displayed. He replied in the same vein that they had custody of our treasures and were displaying them to the best advantage for the world to admire.

At that time, the British Museum had an exhibition on hybrid cultures which included some mummies. They had issued a very advanced form of lighting and many modern techniques to display their artefacts. In one case, they had used X-rays to show us the dentition of the woman who was wrapped in the linen shroud. There were a number of exquisite stone sculptures and wooden objects that told vivid stories of the past.

The Museum has an amazing collection of works, including a stupa from Amravati, images of Hindu gods and goddesses, stone sculptures of the Buddha, bronze figurines and Mughal miniatures. The souvenir shop was full of items that reflected the collection's variety. The merchandise was changed every two or three months. There were special designers hired to produce new and interesting items for sale based on the Museum's many collections.

I visited The Victoria & Albert Museum next. There are 150 galleries here which include the world's best furniture, ceramics, statuary paintings, ornaments and textiles. Of particular interest for Indian visitors is 'Tipu's Tiger', a mechanical figure in which a tiger is shown mauling a British soldier.

The third museum I visited in London was the Tate Modern which has a collection of modern and contemporary art. It has been set up in an abandoned power station. The collection includes almost all the great painters but what impressed me most was the location. I had never seen any structure so large being used as an exhibition space before. When I visited, an artist had created an installation of a boat that was a hundred feet long and thirty feet wide.

This made me think that it would be a fine thing to have such a space in the Bihar Museum to accommodate outsized objects. Other than this, I visited the Natural History Museum, the National Maritime Museum and the National Gallery.

The British Museum hosted me for dinner at a three-star Michelin restaurant. It was rather surprising to learn that Michelin makes tires and yet, it gives its name to an internationally famous system of ranking of food. It has to be said that the food and its presentation were outstanding at that dinner.

Apart from these Museums, I also visited some art galleries. I learned a great deal about how artworks are priced and about art options.

Again, I visited New York as part of the Bihar Museum Project. When I landed in New York it was raining and very cold. By the time the car arrived from the embassy my feet were freezing. The snow was melting and had seeped into my shoes and wet my socks. I realized that my shoes were not going to work in New York and so I expressed the desire to buy new shoes on the way to the hotel. We went to a good shoe shop where I said that I would like to buy a pair of shoes that would protect my feet from the cold for a hundred dollars or less. I got a pair of police boots that hurt my feet when I walked. On hearing this, the shopkeeper said I would have to buy an insole for another thirty-two dollars. I was forced to buy those shoes. It was only then that I could walk around in New York.

Our hotel was in front of the United Nations. The weather was cold and the freezing rain made everything damp. I got ready and left my hotel to go and see Times Square. Along the way, the world's great brands all had set up shops. But there did not seem to be many buyers. I was told that it was a status symbol to have a shop in this area whether there were buyers or not. I was not impressed by Times Square. It was the area from which roads radiated in all directions. Many exhibitions of different art forms were being held there.

One of my New York friends told me that the residents of the city love to go to the opera. He even booked me a ticket. It may be an art form close to the hearts of New Yorkers but I could not take more than an hour of it. It seemed to me that the lighting was very modern.

My first stop in the city was The Museum of Modern Art (MOMA). It is one of the greatest collections of modern and contemporary art. Apart from Henri Rousseau's *The Dream* and Roy Lichtenstein's *Drowning Girl*, the museum has two Picassos, including *Les Demoiselles d'Avignon* and Andy Warhol's *Campbell Soup*. *The Persistence of Memory*, Salvador Dali's most famous painting, is also part of this collection. Apart from its enviable collection of modern and contemporary artists, the museum has an extensive design section featuring some astonishingly designed articles of everyday use. There are tools, furniture, textiles, racing cars and even the design of a helicopter. MOMA has been collecting paintings, sculpture, prints, drawings, photographs, architectural and other designs as well as films since 1929. It has more than two hundred thousand objects.

I also visited the Metropolitan Museum of Art. It is as big as the Louvre and the British Museum with about as many important artworks. We studied the South Asian galleries which has a great collection. We got the opportunity to see how these artworks are presented and rotated from time to time. This Museum also has an important collection of artworks from India. But it's crowning glory, perhaps, is an entire Egyptian temple built during the reign of Augustus Caesar in the first century BCE. This was one of the many temples which were submerged when the Aswan Dam came up on the River Nile and so the Egyptian government offered it to the US. It was dismantled and reconstructed at the Met! The Met also has a fine and extensive collection of Greek and Roman artefacts. Another important collection of modern and contemporary artworks in New York is the Guggenheim whose collection includes many artworks of a high sort.

Like Paris, New York is also an expensive city. These days it is the epicentre of the art world. What Paris once was the world of art and culture, New York is today.

Art is almost entirely about business today, and big business. But it wasn't always so. If one excludes art of the pre-historic age which was executed on the walls of caves, most art, except folk art, was created for the consumption of royalty, the elites and monied gentry. Before the advent of photography, royalty would often commission artworks for churches or temples. Historic pieces would commemorate events now visible in museums. Then portraits began to be commissioned and important people had themselves painted. The advent of photography changed things and modern art was born. Earlier, art was for decoration or to memorialize or remember, now contemporary art is treated as an investment. There are auction houses and galleries in the art business today. The prices of artworks run into millions of dollars. In the language of economics, they are now commodities and like commodities, they are treated as investments by banks and rich people alike. Of course, Christie's and Sotheby's, the premier auctions houses, have been in existence for nearly 200 years. But now they have branches in every important nation; and galleries can be numbered in the thousands.

Exhibitions travel to different countries and critics are an important part of the ecosystem. It is said that art often outperforms land, banks deposits and gold as an investment. The art business is located largely in the developed nations. Two-thirds of the buying and selling of art takes place in the major metropolises of New York, London, Paris, Shanghai and Hong Kong. Clearly, then, the art market thrives where there is money. In the same way, nearly half of India's art market is located in Mumbai and Delhi. And two-thirds of that market is taken up by ten or twelve major artists. Those who do not feature on these lists must struggle to survive.

By studying the art world, it became clear to me that there are not more than a thousand people, auction houses and galleries on the planet that decide the price of an artwork. In the same way, a hundred people can make or break an artist. One of the interesting stories I heard was how the Chinese government bought the works of the artists of China at inflated rates, thus, pushing up the prices. In London, I heard of a gallery that had commissioned an artist to make a work and paid for it. The gallery then went to a collector and got him to pay ten times more for it. The gallery assured the collector that the work would sell for fifty times more in two or three years. And that did happen.

A third route to promote an artist is to have exhibitions in museums or galleries in major metropolises to increase the visibility of the artist. These exhibitions and even their locations act as validation and the price these artworks can command goes up accordingly. It has also been seen that when a gallery or an organization features a lot of artworks by an artist, it can invent a romantic story about his/her struggles and then a documentary or even a book may be produced on the subject. The artist's work is then shown at a gallery, the prices are inflated and investors come in to buy.

9

In the World of Culture and Horticulture

I have always been one with nature. From my childhood, I have been attracted to rivers, waterfalls, mountains and jungles. When I began my career, I was interested in sports and youth programmes. My wife took an interest in plants and gardening and enjoyed using drift wood and rocks to decorate the house. Government houses generally had plenty of land. My wife would immediately get to work on the garden, planting decorative plants. I thought it might be a better idea to grow some vegetables. This could help with our expenses. But after a while I began to enjoy flowers and plants too. I abandoned all opposition and began to take an interest in gardening.

I started my work life in Hazaribagh, which was replete with the beauties of nature. My wife loves pretty gardens, flowers and driftwood. But I felt that the ground around our home would best be used as a productive space where we could grow things to eat and so save some money. But slowly, I came around to her way of thinking. I began to enjoy my visits to the jungle. There too, I would collect specimens to grow. I began to develop a liking for rare succulents. When their colour or shape is different from the run-of-the-mill, they begin to acquire importance and are much more expensive. Collecting rare succulents soon became my passion. When I was posted to Purnia, I would often visit Kalimpong where there were some big nurseries. Some families there who had come from Nepal had valuable experience in growing succulents in cold climates. They had developed contacts with foreign nurseries from whom they got new specimens and varieties.

Kalimpong is cold through the year and receives good rainfall. It has a good tourist traffic which visits Darjeeling too. The tourists also buy these plants giving a fillip to the business of nurseries.

When I was posted in Dhumka, one of its districts was Jamtara. Now, this is a part of Jharkhand. I would visit Jamtara for the weekly court. Jamtara was situated near Chittaranjan City where there is a rail coach factory. There were some good nurseries there too. Some of them were quite old and had good collections. There I was introduced to a collector who imported seeds from abroad and grew plants through tissue culture. He was adept at grafting colourful cactii. Our friendship grew. I would get rare plants from abroad and give him some samples. He would multiply them.

The people of West Bengal also have a deep love of plants and so I also acquired many specimens from there for my collection. There are many old nurseries in Bengal from where I acquired interesting specimens. Calcutta also has some old nurseries. I would make a couple of visits every year and gather specimens. Close to Calcutta, in the village of Makarde, there was a famous collector who had opened a big nursery too. When his health began to fail, he sold me a lot of rare plants at throwaway prices.

My interest in plants grew into a passion. When I went to the Centre on deputation, I became a member of the Indian Cactus and Succulents Society. They have an annual show in Delhi and this is attended in large numbers by the nurseries and collectors all over India. My collection grew rapidly in Delhi since it was easy to import when I was there.

First, I started to collect from Pune, Bangalore, Kalimpong, Hyderabad and Calcutta. Later, when I began to travel abroad, my horizons expanded. I made contact with collectors in other countries. I went on treks in South America, Madagascar and South Africa to collect specimens. These plants are also grown in large numbers in Japan, Thailand and Indonesia. I imported many plants from these countries. Today, I have about 8,000 plants from across the world. In many countries, I abandoned my clothes and books in order to fill my suitcases with plants. The biggest benefits of this passion have been meeting other collectors across the world and sharing information with them. We also exchanged rare plants.

In 1988, I went for a week-long training at Bangalore. It is a city with lots of nurseries. Lal Bagh, one of the famous gardens in the city, hosts a sale of plants by the Nurserymen Association. In the Sidapur area behind Lal Bagh, there are dozens of very old nurseries.

I began to visit these nurseries in the evenings, after the

training was done for the day. I spent two evenings at the most famous of the nurseries, the KSG nursery, learning a great deal from Mr Parthasarthi, its owner. The KSG nursery is about a hundred years old and it has a collection of rare plants from across the world. KSG had been instrumental in introducing many new species to India. Even today, it is famous for its collection of rare plants. One evening when I visited, an official of the TATA group was there too. He intended to buy a rare plant of which KSG only had two specimens, one in the ground and the other in a pot, and which I had been eyeing as well. The TATA official offered twenty thousand rupees for the potted specimen, but Mr Parthasarthi turned down the offer.

Then Mr Parthasarthi asked me how much money I had at that moment. I said I had come on a training and had about three thousand rupees with me. He offered to let me have the potted specimen for that much. On asking him why he had turned down an offer of twenty thousand rupees and was prepared to give me the plant for almost a tenth of that amount, he said, 'I can see how deeply you care about living things.'

This deepened my enthusiasm for rare plants and went a long way in turning it into an obsession.

I found that Bihar was not the best place to grow a variety of species. There are days of great heat. The temperature can shoot up to 40°C and plummet to 10°C in winter, and many plants cannot bear this variation. Plants that need a lot of water and humidity also do not grow well in Bihar. I wanted to start a collection that few people would have but which would also become popular among the public. It also became clear that people were beginning to live in flats, they could not find land to create gardens. They could not find gardeners as well. At some places, there was very little water supply. So I was looking for plants that grow slowly and need little water and less attention.

Succulents seemed an ideal choice; they are small, hardy and need little water. And they are available in many colours and shapes. They can be grown in small pots. I call them the 'plants of tomorrow' because they do not need much room or too many tools to maintain a fine collection. I began with aloe, agave, haworthia, sans evieria and gasteria. They are xerophytes—plants that grow in areas of low rainfall and poor soil. I began to expand my collection to include variegations. Often variations in colour or in form turn up in nature or where there are huge collections in nurseries. These varietals attract attention in the botanical world. They are called variegated or monstrous. The odd thing is that if a human being does not conform to the norm, our gaze is not kind; but in the case of plants, the value increases with 'abnormality'.

I began to show people my collection to make them aware of the beauty of these plants. My son, Apoorva Sukant, has made dozens of videos on these plants which are very popular on YouTube. Some of my writing, dealing with the care and cultivation of these plants, has appeared in the journal of The Indian Society of Cacti and Succulents. Today, our collection is well known across India and my son's company, Scene Scape, is known as a good source of rare plants (www.scenescape.org). He has started online sales to national and international clients. He has many employees and earns well from the venture.

In the World of Culture and Horticulture

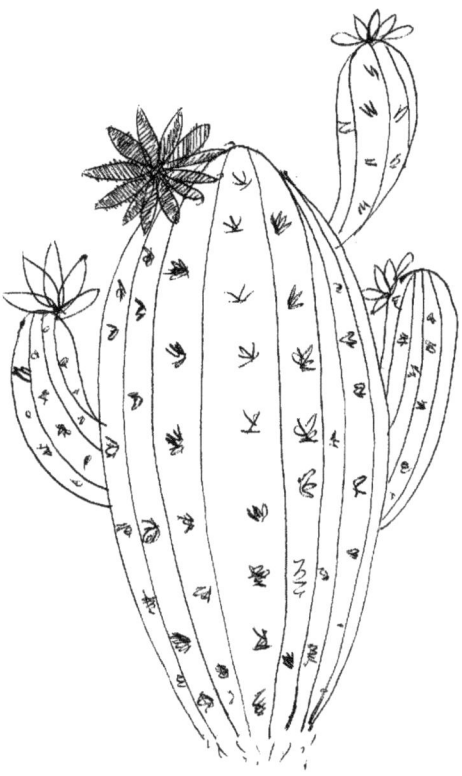

In the last thirty years, my collection has become one of the most important collections of the country. Writers and photographers began to visit me in large numbers. Whenever I went abroad, I would first complete the work for which I had been sent and then visit collectors in that country. The advantage was that I would get these specimens at very low rates and also gather a lot of information about growing them.

I spend about two hours daily with my plants. This is the best time of day for me. I can't quite describe in words how much happiness it gives me when I visit them, talk to them and take care of them. I do not think it is possible to grow these plants by reading a book or getting a degree. One must have a passion for it and get one's hands dirty cleaning up and looking after them oneself. It is only then that they will respond as they should. Most of the books that deal with this come from America and are written for a different climate and environment. India presents a different set of problems.

I do not think it is as useful having someone who has a PhD to look after one's plants as it is to have a person who has ten years of experience actually growing them. Most people feel that in order to achieve something in life or to succeed in an enterprise one needs a high degree of education. But this has not been my experience. There are definite advantages to having an education of course, but natural intelligence and a willingness to learn seem to be pre-requisites for any kind of success in life.

I have put a lot of my time and energy into developing a personal collection of plants. Thanks to my tours of foreign countries and because of the Bihar Museum I could travel abroad and make contact with aficionados of art and culture. Most of the great artists came to Patna on the occasion of the Bihar Museum opening. Many of them became my friends and slowly, I began to build my own art collection. I offered an out-house to artists as a studio for them to use to create their artworks. The majority of the artists who took advantage of this were from Bihar, Jharkhand and Bengal.

Thus, my home has been filled with artworks. I have spent many evenings with these artists when we sat together and discussed their work.

Himmat Shah, one of the greatest artists of India, has a deep love of Bihar. He comes to Bihar regularly and is often heard saying that the next big thing will come from this State. He sees an unquestionable spark in the people of Bihar. When he visits Patna, he comes to stay with me and we stay up talking late into the night about the state of India's art world. He is a man of integrity and also the nation's best sculptor. His clay sculptures are non-paralleled. Shah never married and has no family. Thus, we celebrate his birthday every year at my home to which many contemporary artists are invited. My understanding of art has been hugely enriched by my association with him.

I have always had thousands of specimens of rare plants but now I also have a sizeable collection of art. I wanted to sell my old house and build a new one in which both my passions could find space to be displayed as they should. My old house was in Nava Nagar Colony, Phulwari Sharif and had been built in 1990. I sold this house and land and with the money, bought a property on the Patna-Bihta road, about twenty kilometres away from the city.

I look forward to retiring and running a nursery and creating a small private modern art museum. The house was designed so that we might stay on the ground floor and the two upper storeys could house the museum. Now this house is ready and in a short while, the plants and the artworks will reach their new home. Himmat Shah has become an integral part of our family and so we decided to call this museum The Himmat Shah Museum.

Our family has a tradition of reaching out to help underprivileged students. Wherever we were posted, we were quartered in large bungalows with outhouses for the support staff. We would often make these available for free to students who came to these cities and towns to study but could not afford to pay for accommodation. When I was posted in Patna at the Secretary level, I was allotted a sprawling bungalow. Apart from the very large main house, there were quarters in the compound for at least ten families. Some of these quarters were occupied by the support staff. The remaining were occupied by indigent students of the Patna College of Arts; they also had the benefit of open space for their work, and regular meals. Many of them went on to become famous artists and prosperous too. The benefit to me was that art was being produced every day around my home and I could talk to creative people in the evenings and offer them encouragement. I would also host exhibitions of their works.

When my collection numbered around 400 artworks, including paintings and sculptures, people began to suggest that a book should be published about it. Many art critics of repute expressed an interest in writing the book. Eventually, I chose Alka Pande who is one of the best-known curators. A small book titled *Plural India* was published. Seven famous artists sent in hand-written messages: they were Himmat Shah, Paresh Maity, Manu Parekh, Jatin Das, P. Daroz, Jyoti Bhatt and Arpana Caur. The book was praised in art circles. People found there was much variety in my collection. I dedicated the book to Nitish Kumar, the Bihar Chief Minister, since it was because of him that I got an opportunity to do such important work in the field of art.

10

Friends Forever

Friends are an important part of one's life. Some friends we make while we are studying, others share our interests. Some friendships arise out of a shared work situation.

In the village, my close friends as a child included Surendra Sinha, Vishwanath Sahni Ramsagar Mahto, Shailesh and Uday. They were all good at studies. Surendra was my rival at studies. Every day, we met by the banks of the Baya River and told each other lies. He would say I didn't study at all because I got caught up in listening to the radio or I fell asleep, etc. Later on, Vishwanath became a teacher and Ramsagar became a junior engineer. Shailesh became a headmaster and Uday, a railway guard. Surendra's life was cut short.

At Patna College, my friends included Kashinath Shukla, Ranvir, Jaikaran Prasad and Niranjan Sinha. Kashinath retired as the Section Officer of Patna High Court. I built my first house on Ranvir's father's property. He did not want to sell me the land as they had plenty but I could not accept it as a gift and eventually we accepted a rate that was somewhat lower than the market price. Jaikaran became the Treasury Officer of Jharkhand. Ranvir is no longer with us. At JNU, Anil Oza was a friend; he joined the police force.

The IAS offers a variety of postings, jobs and contact with different kinds of people. I got the opportunity to work in various settings and with different types of people. Some of them became close friends. Each year, about a hundred new entrants to the IAS become batchmates. Since training happens together there are many opportunities for bonding. One also gets a chance to meet or make contact with people from all corners of the country. One also has the opportunity to make friends when one travels within the country or abroad.

I had many chances in my career to expand the circle of my friends. Many people feel that you should change your friends circle over time. They believe that to climb the ladder of success you must leave behind friends who have not risen with you. I have never agreed with this philosophy. Most of the people whom I have befriended are still in touch with me. My friends include people from all castes and communities. Although you tend to meet people of your own community more often, I have always tried to take everyone with me. We celebrated the silver jubilee of our friendship at Patna College and had a great time remembering the good old days.

At college, I had friends from all castes and communities. We formed deep and lasting bonds. They all spread out later and did a variety of jobs. Some started businesses. In those days, people valued friendship over family.

As part of the IAS, one had many duties and

responsibilities and it is true that this often makes finding time for family difficult. I had two or three ideas in my head when I started out. The first was that I should make full use of all the opportunities that my time in the service brought me. I was assigned to the Bihar cadre. I decided to devote my time and energy to my State. In comparison to other States, Bihar was considered under-developed and backward. And so there were opportunities to work in different areas. My interests lay in rural development, women's empowerment, education, sports and art and culture. I made the best of my time in these departments. I could never be a nine-to-five bureaucrat. I was not interested in the creation and maintenance of files.

I have always regretted not having found time for my family. However, in one sense, one might say that all of Bihar became my family. In all that I did, my wife provided unstinting support, nearly single-handedly bringing up the children and keeping the house in good order. Another good thing was that we all had our own interests. My wife enjoyed gardening, handicrafts and ensuring that the children had a good education. Since she taught in a university, she got an opportunity to work closely with children and the youth.

Teaching in the Bihar universities was not what it once was. There were very few teachers who came on time and held their classes and since there were very few classes only a handful of students bothered to attend lectures. My wife was a disciplinarian. However, her classes were always full. My son had a fondness for science and technology and so after he got a degree in science, he continued to be interested in technology. My daughter was fond of dance and singing and all of us had deep interests that kept us going. My wife insisted that we should all eat together at least once a day so we could catch up as a family. However, this does not happen as often as it should. Our best times together have been outside Patna when we have gone together on a trip.

The journey of my life began in Chamtha and took me to Patna. Then I spent a little time in Delhi. I travelled to a few countries; I have climbed mountains and trekked in forests. I have met thousands of people for work and as a tourist. I made many friends along the way and yet, it is the succulents whom I would count among my best friends. I enjoy the time I spend looking after them, watering them, talking to them, just being with them. Art and artists also have a very special place in my life and so my journey continues.

ALSO FROM SPEAKING TIGER

IN THE SERVICE OF FREE INDIA
MEMOIR OF A CIVIL SERVANT
B.D. Pande

A fascinating and historically significant recollection of a life lived in the service of a newly liberated India.

In the decades following 1947, as the tallest national leaders were building a new India, they were supported by a band of idealistic civil servants fiercely committed to the country's Constitution and its people. Among these remarkable officers was Bhairab Datt Pande, a young man from the Himalayan district of Kumaon, who joined the Indian Civil Service in 1939. Over almost forty years as civil servant, and later as governor, he played an important role in the country's administration, and interacted with leaders like Indira Gandhi (as cabinet secretary during the Emergency), Morarji Desai and Jyoti Basu. His memoir—which, respecting his wish, is being published posthumously—is a fascinating record of his own life and that of India in the half century after Independence.

Pande chronicles several landmark events and initiatives that he either participated in or witnessed. He helped increase food-grain allotment to the state as food commissioner of Bihar in the early 1950s and drew up a new famine code as land reforms commissioner. His work in the Community Development programme some years later still has important lessons for today's Panchayati Raj institutions. After retirement, he was governor of West Bengal during the resurgence of Naxalism in the early 1980s, and of Punjab in 1983-84—a tragic and turbulent year in the history of the state and the nation. Pande chose to resign as governor rather than carry out unconstitutional orders. His compelling narration of the behind-the-scenes events and negotiations leading up to the Anandpur Sahib Resolution and Operation Bluestar is of great value.

Engaging and inspiring in equal measure, this memoir is both a fascinating record of an extraordinary life and an important and revealing historical document.

ALSO FROM SPEAKING TIGER

A LUXURY CALLED HEALTH
A DOCTOR'S JOURNEY THROUGH THE ART, THE SCIENCE AND THE TRICKERY OF MEDICINE

Kavery Nambisan

The miracles and tragedies of life, the compassion and cruelties of humanity are nowhere more visible than in the field of medicine. It is these that Kavery Nambisan—doctor and writer of immense sensitivity—explores in this memoir, drawing upon her work over four decades in rural and small-town India.

Through her patients' stories, she depicts the highs and lows of medical practice: Sudha, in Mokama, Bihar, left immobilized waist-down after being set on fire by her in-laws, but determined to walk; construction workers in Lonavala, Maharashtra, who prefer the quick-fix of the 'drip', so that they won't miss their daily wage; four-year-old Pavana in the Anamallais, mauled by a leopard, who had to be driven over 40 kilometres of gutted roads to the nearest hospital. And in contrast, the friend of a Tamil Nadu chief minister who could summon a doctor repeatedly, at will, to attend to her stubbed toe. Settled in Kodagu, Karnataka, after years of practice as a surgeon, Kavery now works as a GP, and she writes about treating snake bites, skin diseases, tuberculosis, epileptic seizures and Covid-19 infections, even as she examines the state of public health in India.

Engaging, incisive and deeply felt, *A Luxury Called Health* shows, as few books have done, 'the sincerity and the deception, the valour and the cowardice beneath the white coat'.

www.ingramcontent.com/pod-product-compliance
Lightning Source LLC
LaVergne TN
LVHW041907070526
838199LV00051BA/2539